Reach the Highest Standard
in Professional Learning: Outcomes

Volumes in the Reach the Highest Standard in Professional Learning Series

Learning Communities

Leadership

Resources

Data

Learning Designs

Implementation

Outcomes

Reach the Highest Standard in Professional Learning: Outcomes

Delores B. Lindsey

Randall B. Lindsey

Shirley M. Hord

Valerie von Frank

A Joint Publication

CORWIN
A SAGE Company

*learning*forward

CORWIN
A SAGE Company

FOR INFORMATION:

Corwin

A SAGE Company

2455 Teller Road

Thousand Oaks, California 91320

(800) 233-9936

www.corwin.com

SAGE Publications Ltd.

1 Oliver's Yard

55 City Road

London EC1Y 1SP

United Kingdom

SAGE Publications India Pvt. Ltd.

B 1/I 1 Mohan Cooperative Industrial Area

Mathura Road, New Delhi 110 044

India

SAGE Publications Asia-Pacific Pte. Ltd.

3 Church Street

#10-04 Samsung Hub

Singapore 049483

Printed in the United States of America

A catalog record of this book is available from the Library of Congress.

ISBN 978-1-4522-9195-6

This book is printed on acid-free paper.

Acquisitions Editor: Dan Alpert

Associate Editor: Kimberly Greenberg

Editorial Assistant: Cesar Reyes

Production Editor: Amy Schroller

Copy Editor: Janet Ford

Typesetter: C&M Digitals (P) Ltd.

Proofreader: Liann Lech

Indexer: Sheila Bodell

Cover Designer: Gail Buschman

Marketing Manager: Stephanie Trkay

Certified Chain of Custody
SUSTAINABLE FORESTRY INITIATIVE
Promoting Sustainable Forestry
www.sfiprogram.org
SFI-01268
SFI label applies to text stock

15 16 17 18 19 10 9 8 7 6 5 4 3 2 1

Contents

Introduction to the Series

These are the demands on educators and school systems right now, among many others:

- They must fulfill the moral imperative of educating every child for tomorrow's world, regardless of background or status.
- They must be prepared to implement college- and career-ready standards and related assessments.
- They must implement educator evaluations tied to accountability systems.

A critical element in creating school systems that can meet these demands is building the capacity of the system's educators at all levels, from the classroom teacher to the instructional coach to the school principal to the central office administrator, and including those partners who work within and beyond districts. Building educator capacity in this context requires effective professional learning.

Learning Forward's Standards for Professional Learning define the essential elements of and conditions for professional learning that leads to changed educator practices and improved student results. They are grounded in the understanding that the ultimate purpose of professional learning is increasing student success. Educator effectiveness—and this includes all educators working in and with school systems, not just teachers—is linked closely to student learning. Therefore, increasing the effectiveness of educators is a key lever to school improvement.

Effective professional learning happens in a culture of continuous improvement, informed by data about student and educator performance and supported by leadership and sufficient resources.

Educators learning daily have access to information about relevant instructional strategies and resources and, just as important, time for collaboration with colleagues, coaches, and school leaders. Education leaders and systems that value effective professional learning not only provide sufficient time and money but also create structures that reinforce monitoring and evaluation of that learning so they understand what is effective and have information to adjust and improve.

WHY STANDARDS?

Given that any system can—and must—develop expertise about professional learning, why are standards important? Among many reasons are these:

First, adherence to standards ensures equity. When learning leaders across schools and systems agree to follow a common set of guidelines, they are committing to equal opportunities for all the learners in those systems. If all learning is in alignment with the Standards for Professional Learning and tied to student and school improvement goals, then all educators have access to the best expertise available to improve their practice and monitor results.

Standards also provide a common language that allows for conversation, collaboration, and implementation planning that crosses state, regional, and national borders. This collaboration can leverage expertise from any corner of the world to change practice and results.

Finally, standards offer guidelines for accountability. While an endorsement of the standards doesn't in itself guarantee quality, they provide a framework within which systems can establish measures to monitor progress, alignment, and results.

FROM STANDARDS TO TRANSFORMATION

So a commitment to standards is a first critical step. Moving into deep understanding and sustained implementation of standards is another matter. Transforming practices, and indeed, whole systems, will require long-term study, planning, and evaluation.

Reach the Highest Standard in Professional Learning is created to be an essential set of tools to help school and system leaders take those steps. As with the Standards for Professional Learning themselves, there will be seven volumes, one for each standard.

While the standards were created to work in synergy, we know that educators approach professional learning from a wide range of experiences, concerns, expertise, and passions. Perhaps a school leader may have started PLCs in his school to address a particular learning challenge, and thus has an abiding interest in how learning communities can foster teacher quality and better results. Maybe a central office administrator started her journey to standards-based professional learning through a study of how data inform changes, and she wants to learn more about the foundations of data use. This series was created to support such educators and to help them continue on their journey of understanding systemwide improvement and the pieces that make such transformation possible.

In developing this series of books on the Standards for Professional Learning, Corwin and Learning Forward envisioned that practitioners would enter this world of information through one particular book, and that their needs and interests would take them to all seven as the books are developed. The intention is to serve the range of needs practitioners bring and to support a full understanding of the elements critical to effective professional learning.

All seven volumes in Reach the Highest Standard in Professional Learning share a common structure, with components to support knowledge development, exploration of changes in practice, and a vision of each concept at work in real-world settings.

In each volume, readers will find

- A think piece developed by a leading voice in the professional learning field. These thought leaders represent both scholars and practitioners, and their work invites readers to consider the foundations of each standard and to push understanding of those seven standards.
- An implementation piece that helps readers put the think piece and related ideas into practice, with tools for both individuals and groups to use in reflection and discussion about the standards. Shirley M. Hord and Patricia Roy, series editors and longstanding Learning Forward standards leaders, created the implementation pieces across the entire series.
- A case study that illuminates what it looks like in schools and districts when education leaders prioritize the standards in

their improvement priorities. Valerie von Frank, with many years of writing about education in general and professional learning in particular, reported these pieces, highlighting insights specific to each standard.

MOVING TOWARD TRANSFORMATION

We know this about effective professional learning: Building awareness isn't enough to change practice. It's a critical first piece, and these volumes will help in knowledge development. But sustaining knowledge and implementing change require more.

Our intention is that the content and structure of the volumes can move readers from awareness to changes in practice to transformation of systems. And of course transformation requires much more. Commitment to a vision for change is an exciting place to start. A long-term informed investment of time, energy, and resources is non-negotiable, as is leadership that transcends one visionary leader who will inevitably move on.

Ultimately, it will be the development of a culture of collective responsibility for all students that sustains improvement. We invite you to begin your journey toward developing that culture through study of the Standards for Professional Learning and through Reach the Highest Standard in Professional Learning. Learning Forward will continue to support the development of knowledge, tools, and evidence that inform practitioners and the field. Next year's challenges may be new ones, and educators working at their full potential will always be at the core of reaching our goals for students.

Stephanie Hirsh
Executive Director, Learning Forward

The Learning Forward Standards for Professional Learning

Learning Communities: Professional learning that increases educator effectiveness and results for all students occurs within learning communities committed to continuous improvement, collective responsibility, and goal alignment.

Leadership: Professional learning that increases educator effectiveness and results for all students requires skillful leaders who develop capacity, advocate, and create support systems for professional learning.

Resources: Professional learning that increases educator effectiveness and results for all students requires prioritizing, monitoring, and coordinating resources for educator learning.

Data: Professional learning that increases educator effectiveness and results for all students uses a variety of sources and types of student, educator, and system data to plan, assess, and evaluate professional learning.

Learning Designs: Professional learning that increases educator effectiveness and results for all students integrates theories, research, and models of human learning to achieve its intended outcomes.

Implementation: Professional learning that increases educator effectiveness and results for all students applies research on change and sustains support for implementation of professional learning for long-term change.

Outcomes: Professional learning that increases educator effectiveness and results for all students aligns its outcomes with educator performance and student curriculum standards.

Source: Learning Forward. (2011). *Standards for professional learning.* Oxford, OH: Author.

The Outcomes Standard

Professional learning that increases educator effectiveness and results for all students aligns its outcomes with educator performance and student curriculum standards.

For all students to learn, educators and professional learning must be held to high standards. Professional learning that increases results for all students addresses the learning outcomes and performance expectations education systems designate for students and educators. When the content of professional learning integrates student curriculum and educator performance standards, the link between educator learning and student learning becomes explicit, increasing the likelihood that professional learning contributes to increased student learning. When systems increase the stakes for students by demanding high, equitable outcomes, the stakes for professional learning increase as well.

MEET PERFORMANCE STANDARDS

Educator performance standards typically delineate the knowledge, skills, practices, and dispositions of highly effective educators. Standards guide preparation, assessment, licensing, induction, practice, and evaluation. Frequently regulated by government agencies, standards establish requirements for educator preparation, define expectations of an effective workforce, guide career-long professional learning of the education workforce, and set fair and reliable indicators of effectiveness for measuring educator performance.

Teacher standards specify what teachers need to know and do to deliver on the promise of an effective, equitable education for every student. Typical areas included in teacher standards are knowledge, skills, and dispositions related to content knowledge; pedagogy; pedagogical content knowledge; assessment; understanding how students learn; understanding how students' cognitive, social, emotional, and physical development influences their learning; engaging students with diverse cultures, language, gender, socioeconomic conditions, and exceptionalities; engaging families and communities in student learning; and creating learning environments, professional growth and development, and professional collaboration.

Standards for school and system leaders, like teacher standards, describe what effective leaders know and do so that every student and educator performs at high levels. Whether for teacher leaders or school or school system administrators, these standards delineate specific expectations for preparation, assessment, licensure, professional learning, practice, and evaluation of those engaged in leadership roles within a school or school system. Typical areas covered in leader standards include establishing a vision and strategic plan for effective learning; leading learning of students and staff; developing workplace culture to support learning; engaging in their own professional learning; managing facilities, workforce, operations, and resources; establishing effective relationships and communication systems; managing change; sharing leadership with others; engaging staff and families in decision making; understanding and responding to the diverse needs of students and communities; understanding and responding to cultural, political, social, legal, and financial contexts; and securing individual, team, school, and whole system accountability for student success.

Standards for other members of the education workforce delineate the unique knowledge, skills, qualities, and dispositions required of those in specialized roles. These roles include school nurses, guidance counselors, librarians, instructional coaches, resource personnel, classroom assistants, and other instructional and non-instructional staff who are vital to schools and school systems. Standards for advanced or specialized certification guide professional learning for those who seek career advancement or differentiated roles.

ADDRESS LEARNING OUTCOMES

Student learning outcomes define equitable expectations for all students to achieve at high levels and hold educators responsible for implementing appropriate strategies to support student learning. Learning for educators that focuses on student learning outcomes has a positive effect on changing educator practice and increasing student achievement. Whether the learning outcomes are developed locally or nationally and are defined in content standards, courses of study, curriculum, or curricular programs, these learning outcomes serve as the core content for educator professional learning to support effective implementation and results. With student learning outcomes as the focus, professional learning deepens educators' content knowledge, pedagogical content knowledge, and understanding of how students learn the specific discipline. Using student learning outcomes as its outcomes, professional learning can model and engage educators in practices they are expected to implement within their classrooms and workplaces.

BUILD COHERENCE

Coherence requires that professional learning builds on what educators have already learned; focuses on learning outcomes and pedagogy aligned with national or local curriculum and assessments for educator and student learning; aligns with educator performance standards; and supports educators in developing sustained, ongoing professional communication with other educators who are engaged in similar changes in their practice. Any single professional learning activity is more likely to be effective in improving educator performance and student learning if it builds on earlier professional learning and is followed up with later, more advanced work to become a part of a coherent set of opportunities for ongoing professional learning. Coherence also ensures that professional learning is a part of a seamless process that begins in the preparation program, continues throughout an educator's career, and aligns tightly with the expectations for effectiveness defined in performance standards and student learning outcomes.

Source: Learning Forward. (2011). *Standards for professional learning.* Oxford, OH: Author.

About the Authors

Delores B. Lindsey, PhD, a recently retired Associate Professor from California State University, San Marcos, has also served as a middle grades and high school teacher, assistant principal, principal, and county office administrator. Her primary focus is developing and supporting culturally proficient leaders. Using the lens of Cultural Proficiency, Delores helps educational leaders examine their organization's policies and practices as well as their individual beliefs and values about cross-cultural communication. Her message to her audiences focuses on nurturing socially just educational practices, developing culturally proficient leadership practices, and using diversity as an asset and resource. Delores is coauthor of *Culturally Proficient Instruction: A Guide for People Who Teach*, 3rd ed. (2012), *Culturally Proficient Coaching: Supporting Educators to Create Equitable Schools* (2007), *Culturally Proficient Learning Communities: Confronting Inequities Through Collaborative Inquiry* (2009) and *A Culturally Proficient Response to the Common Core: Ensuring Equity Through Professional Learning* (2015). Delores facilitates educators to develop their own inquiry and action research. She relies on the power of story and storytelling to enhance learning experiences. She asks reflective questions and encourages group members to use questions as prompts for their organizational stories. Her favorite reflective questions are: *Who are we?* and *Are we who we say we are?*

 **Randall B. Lindsey,** PhD, is Emeritus Professor, California State University, Los Angeles, and has a practice centered on educational consulting and issues related to equity and access. Prior to higher education faculty roles, Randy served as a junior and senior high school history teacher, a district office administrator for school desegregation, and executive director of a nonprofit corporation. All of Randy's experiences have been in working with diverse populations, and his area of study is the behavior of white people in multicultural settings. It is his belief and experience that too often members of dominant groups are observers of cross-cultural issues rather than personally involved with them. He works with colleagues to design and implement programs for and with schools and community-based organizations to provide access and achievement.

With coauthors Kikanza Nuri Robins and Raymond Terrell, he published the initial Cultural Proficiency book, *Cultural Proficiency: A Manual for School Leaders,* now in its 3rd edition (2009) for Corwin. His most recent books, also with Corwin, include *Culturally Proficient Collaboration: The Use and Misuse of School Counselors* (with Diana L. Stephens, 2011); an edited volume *The Best of Corwin: Equity* (2012); *Culturally Proficient Practice: Supporting Educators of English Learning Students* (with Reyes Quezada and Delores Lindsey, 2012); and *A Culturally Proficient Response to the Common Core: Ensuring Equity Through Professional Learning* (with Delores B. Lindsey, Karen M. Kearney, Delia Estrada, and Raymond D. Terrell, 2015). Randall will publish a chapter titled "Culturally Proficient Leadership: Doing What's Right for Students—All Students" (with coauthor Raymond Terrell, 2015) in *Key Questions for Educational Leaders* edited by John P. Portelli and Darrin Griffiths and published by Words and Deeds. Randy and his wife and frequent coauthor, Delores, are enjoying this phase of life as grandparents, as educators, and in support of just causes that extend the promises of democracy throughout society in authentic ways.

 **Dr. Shirley M. Hord**, PhD, is the Scholar Laureate of Learning Forward (previously National Staff Development Council), following her retirement as Scholar Emerita at the Southwest Educational Development Laboratory in Austin, Texas. There she directed the Strategies for Increasing Student Success Program. She continues to design and coordinate professional development activities related to educational change and improvement, school leadership, and the creation of professional learning communities.

Her early roles as elementary school classroom teacher and university science education faculty at The University of Texas at Austin were followed by her appointment as co-director of Research on the Improvement Process at the Research and Development Center for Teacher Education at The University of Texas at Austin. There she administered and conducted research on school improvement and the role of school leaders in school change.

She served as a fellow of the National Center for Effective Schools Research and Development and was U.S. representative to the Foundation for the International School Improvement Project, an international effort that develops research, training, and policy initiatives to support local school improvement practices. In addition to working with educators at all levels across the United States and Canada, Hord makes presentations and consults in Asia, Europe, Australia, Africa, and Mexico.

Her current interests focus on the creation and functioning of educational organizations as learning communities and the role of leaders who serve such organizations. Dr. Hord is the author of numerous articles and books, of which a selection of the most recent are *Implementing Change: Patterns, Principles, and Potholes,* 4th ed. (with Gene E. Hall, 2015); *Reclaiming Our Teaching Profession: The Power of Educators Learning in Community* (with Edward F. Tobia, 2012); and *A Playbook for Professional Learning: Putting the Standards Into Action* (with Stephanie Hirsh, 2012).

Valerie von Frank is an author, editor, and communications consultant. A former newspaper editor and education reporter, she has focused much of her writing on education issues, including professional learning. She served as communications director in an urban school district and a nonprofit school reform organization and was the editor for 7 years of *JSD,* the flagship magazine for the National Staff Development Council, now Learning Forward. She has written extensively for education publications, including *JSD, Tools for Schools, The Learning System, The Learning Principal,* and *T3.* She is coauthor with Ann Delehant of *Making Meetings Work: How to Get Started, Get Going, and Get It Done* (Corwin, 2007); with Linda Munger of *Change, Lead, Succeed* (National Staff Development Council, 2010); with Robert Garmston of *Unlocking Group Potential to Improve Schools* (Corwin, 2012); and with Jennifer Abrams of *The Multigenerational Workplace: Communicate, Collaborate, and Create Community* (Corwin, 2014).

CHAPTER ONE

Professional Learning Standards Through the Lens of Cultural Proficiency

A Response for Equitable Outcomes

Delores B. Lindsey

Randall B. Lindsey

> *Knowing who your students are and knowing their stories tells the students that you care about them as people, inside and outside of class.*
>
> —Sean Slade, Academic Director, ACSD

The *Standards for Professional Learning* were developed and tested over time for the purpose of outlining characteristics that promote effective professional learning, supportive leadership, and improved student results (Learning Forward, 2014). An important assumption held by the writers of this chapter is that we believe the standards address the professional learning of educators and, as such, involve teachers and administrators invested in their *collaborative* professional learning. Although the professional learning

1

standards are designed to work interdependently, this chapter specifically addresses the Outcomes Standard:

Professional learning that increases educator effectiveness and results for all students aligns its outcomes with educator performance and student curriculum standards.

Briefly summarized, the three "big ideas" embedded within the Outcomes Standard that drive the work of school and district professional learning educators are these deliverables:

- Meet performance standards—achieves knowledge, skills, practices, and dispositions expected of effective educators and are ensured by state licensing agencies and professional associations.
- Address learning outcomes—provides professional learning focused on educator practice and expectations found in pedagogy, educator content knowledge, and understanding how students learn.
- Build coherence—ensures the successful integration of educator knowledge, educator professional standards, and local and/or national assessments aligned with learning outcomes and pedagogy.

We use the lens of Cultural Proficiency to highlight the equity theme embedded in the standard. Equity of access and outcomes for students must be intentionally addressed through professional learning. Figure 1.1 depicts the manner in which Cultural Proficiency frames the three big ideas of the Outcomes Standard.

Cultural Proficiency is an approach to equity and access for all learners. When professional learning is viewed through the equity and access lens of Cultural Proficiency, as depicted in Figure 1.1, coherence toward best practices and high-quality instruction provides all learners with opportunities to be prepared for college and the workplace.

In this publication we focus on educator effectiveness and student performance outcomes through raising equity and access to a level of collective mindfulness. Our assumption, built on sound practice, is that equitable professional learning experiences aligned with professional learning standards and student performance goals support equitable learning outcomes for educators and their students.

Figure 1.1   Interdependent Relationship of Quality Professional
Learning Delivered Through Cultural Proficiency Lens

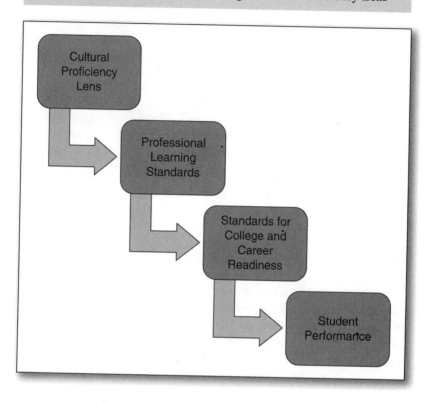

To guide your reading, this chapter has been constructed in seven distinct parts, each of which scaffolds on the preceding parts and often loops back to provide connections, explanations, and illustrations:

1. Organization of the Chapter—describes processes and major content sources.

2. Deeper Attention to Equity and Access—introduces concept of *inside-out* change as both individual and systemic for attaining access and equity outcomes in schools.

3. Mindful Use of the Tools of Cultural Proficiency—uses time-honored communication skills of reflection and dialogue to uncover assumptions and beliefs that guide personal behavior and school policies and practices.

4. Leadership for Systemic Change and Connection—illustrates value and use of continuous improvement within classrooms as well as across schools and districts.

5. Learning Communities as Collaboration-In-Action: Disturbing the System—demonstrates value of learning communities using disaggregated access and achievement data for continuous improvement.

6. Cultural Proficiency: Context and Conditions for Professional Learning—lays out the Tools of Cultural Proficiency in ways that illustrate the necessity for core values that must be visible in the actions of educators and their schools and districts.

7. Planning for Professional Learning—provides a linear path for developing action plans in the dynamic and fluid settings of our schools.

ORGANIZATION OF THE CHAPTER

This chapter is organized to provide a description of the Tools of Cultural Proficiency in the context of Learning Forward's Outcomes Standard. Tables are embedded throughout the chapter to describe the tools, to illustrate use of the tools, and to provide opportunity for your planning to apply the tools to your work. Intermittently, you are provided opportunity to reflect both on your reading and on your practice.

We invite you to use this chapter as a guide for examining your practice as well as the prevalent practices in your school or district that inform professional learning with particular attention to student outcomes. With this chapter you have the opportunity

- to clarify your personal values, assumptions, and beliefs about providing all demographic/cultural groups of students access to high-quality education;
- to develop knowledge and skills for working with fellow educators in developing shared values for educating all demographic groups of students;
- to develop knowledge and skills for creating policies and practices that align with shared values for educating all demographic groups of students; and
- to choose to act differently when you acquire and develop knowledge and skills that make a difference in your life and in the members of your learning community.

By concentrating our individual and collective attention on student access to high-level educational opportunities, we must directly address historical disparities that persist between and among demographic groups of students. Meeting the academic needs of historically marginalized students is an iterative, step-by-step process that calls on educators to engage in two processes:

- To examine our assumptions and beliefs about students, and
- To examine school policies and practices that may unknowingly and unwittingly contribute to disparate treatment in areas such as suspensions, expulsions, assignments to special education, and underrepresentation in high-order curricular opportunities.

Inequity and lack of access become hidden, unexplained assumptions among educators, yet they are accepted unless we are willing to have a deeper conversation about the shared meaning of how our education organizations are meant to serve all students within our school communities.

DEEPER ATTENTION TO EQUITY AND ACCESS

Terry Cross, the executive director of the National Indian Child Welfare Association in Portland, Oregon (1989), describes cultural proficiency as an *inside-out process* of personal and organizational change to foster socially just ends. As such, cultural proficiency is a lens through which educators frame their personal and professional learning for developing core values that guide our personal behaviors and, in turn, the policies and practices of our schools.

As an intentional and mindful inside-out process, cultural proficiency provides the opportunity for each of us to be a student of our own assumptions. Engaging in this inside-out process enables us to learn about assumptions we have made about self, others, and the context in which we work with others. When we extend this inside-out process to a school setting—grade level or department—we function as a learning community by examining the manner in which our assumptions become institutionalized as policies and practices. This deeper use of learning communities takes us closer to personalizing and deprivatizing our practices and actions to assist us in changing the way we talk, plan, act, and engage with colleagues and students who are culturally different from ourselves.

We have been developing the theory and practice of cultural proficiency for two decades and find that the Tools of Cultural Proficiency are an elemental part of the *all students* component of the Outcomes Standard. Just as our students are on their developmental path in all areas of schools' curricula, educators are also moving along a developmental continuum in their knowledge, skills, and dispositions for addressing equitable opportunities and outcomes. The Learning Forward's Outcomes Standard places the responsibility for "growing" educators focused on high-quality, performance-based education for all learners squarely on the shoulders of today's professional learning community. Members of the professional learning community must be mindful of the educational and equity gaps that continue to exist and that were not addressed by previous reform efforts.

In today's richly diverse classrooms, educators are compelled to develop new approaches and acquire new skills while at the same time learn to connect with the students in their classrooms in new and different ways (Pappano, 2010; Wilmore, 2002). For some educators, these behaviors required a shift in thinking from the traditional "subject-based curriculum" approach to a learner-centered, standards-based approach (Armstrong, Henson, & Savage, 2005; Voltz, Sims, & Nelson, 2010). Although the national attention has been on standards-based instruction for well over a decade, many instructors and educational leaders have yet to embrace the shift from a traditional teaching approach to a standards-based instructional model.

Today's complex classrooms and the introduction of the college and career readiness standards require instructors to not only rethink their prior *mental model* for teaching, but to change their ways of determining learner outcomes, preparing lessons, selecting materials, presenting lessons, and assessing learner performance. College and career readiness standards require educators to align the new educational policies (every student should be college and career ready by 12th grade) with the curriculum, instructional practices, and the assessment tools and strategies for 21st century learners. Linked to these alignments are the assumptions and needs for inclusion, collaboration, resources, leadership, and professional learning for diverse school communities. To successfully implement the college and career readiness standards, school district policymakers, administrators, teachers, and community members must recognize that one of the barriers they will confront is a general resistance to change by educators and community members. Overcoming these change barriers requires leaders who are willing to confront student and community inequities and any lack of student access to resources that can support their successes. Often, exposing inequities is just the first step in supporting change initiatives.

Confront

Access and achievement gaps have been made public in ways not envisioned just a few years ago. In their mission statements or statement of core values, most schools and school districts promise "to educate all students to high levels." Similar well-intended phrases and sentiments are ubiquitous in educational settings and are impotent when the chronic underachievement of readily identifiable cultural groups of students continues to be ignored and gaps in access and achievement persist in our schools. Encouragingly, our current national commitment to accountability is taking away the option of continuing to ignore underachievement.

Most states in the United States, the provinces in Canada, and the U.S. government have reform efforts (e.g., No Child Left Behind in the United States and Ontario, Canada's Renewed Vision program) that have at least begun to put the spotlight on chronic areas of student underachievement. Even with the limitations that those pieces of legislation possess, they have one irrefutable common denominator; namely, they have drawn attention to a fact of chronic underachievement that has been present for generations. It is our observation that learning communities and the Tools of Cultural, Proficiency provide principles and tools that we educators can use to direct our professional resources to benefit an ever-widening proportion of the children and youth in our schools.

attention

Cultural Proficiency is about serving the needs of all students, with laser-like focus on historically underserved students. When education is delivered in a culturally proficient manner, historically underserved students gain access to educational opportunities intended to result in high academic achievement. When education is delivered in a culturally proficient manner all students understand and value their own culture and the cultures of those around them. In the same vein, when educational experiences are delivered in a culturally proficient manner, all educators, legislators, board members, and local business community members understand and value the culture of those around them in ways they have rarely experienced or appreciated. Culturally Proficient Professional Learning focuses on learner outcomes as described in Learning Forward's Outcome Standard. Professional learning aligned with educator effectiveness/standards

w/c
ALL
Understand

and focused on student standards/performance takes into consideration the student's culture, learning style, and academic need. Clearly
stated outcomes with a system for monitoring and benchmarking
ensure equitable student results.

For first-time readers of Cultural Proficiency, we provide an over-
view of terms and tools. For those familiar with Cultural Proficiency,
this section serves as a refresher to the terms and tools. An in-depth
description of the Four Tools of Cultural Proficiency is in the section
that follows. The four Tools of Cultural Proficiency that guide our
work are:

- Overcoming the Barriers to Cultural Proficiency—the recognition that systems of historical oppression continue to exist
  and can be overcome by people and organizations that adapt
  their values, behaviors, policies, and practices to meet the
  needs of underserved cultural groups using the democratic
  means of public education.
- The Guiding Principles of Cultural Proficiency—an inclusive
  set of core values that identify the centrality of culture in our
  lives and in our society.
- The Cultural Proficiency Continuum—six points along a continuum to indicate unhealthy and healthy ways of responding
  to cultural difference.
- The Five Essential Elements of Cultural Competence—five
  standards to guide a person's values and behaviors and a
  school/district's policies and practices in meeting the academic needs of cultural groups.

To learn and apply the tools to one's practice and, in turn, to use
the Tools of Cultural Proficiency to frame professional learning with
and for colleagues requires effective communication skills. Reflection
and dialogue are communication and problem-solving skills generally familiar to most educators that, when used skillfully, provide
in-depth personal and professional community learning.

LEADERSHIP FOR
SYSTEMIC CHANGE AND CONNECTIONS

Culturally proficient school leaders know how to work with formal
and non-formal leaders within schools and across school districts. At
the formal level, district- and site-level administrators embrace their

primary function of exerting moral leadership for the district and its schools. Within this context, non-formal leaders are valued and supported at school and classroom levels.

Establishing a culturally proficient school is a journey that begins with those in formal leadership positions closely examining school policies, practices, and procedures to ensure they are aligned in ways that students and community members are afforded equitable access to all areas of the curriculum. School leaders deeply consider the school and/or district's core values to ensure that espoused values are inclusive of the diversity of the community and embrace the assets brought by those cultural and demographic groups.

From Design to Delivery—Continuous Improvement

Cultural Proficiency provides the equity lens for college and career readiness standards so that this new initiative stays focused on *college AND career readiness* rather than risk becoming *college OR career readiness*. We offer you and your colleagues the opportunity to develop a Culturally Proficient Professional Learning Plan as a lens to support implementation of equitable college and career readiness standards in your school and classroom.

Professional learning that supports implementation planning begins at the design stage using a new or alternative curriculum and includes the delivery of that curriculum content (i.e., instructional strategies) and assessment of student progress to inform improvement of instruction. Once again we examine Figure 1.1 as it illustrates the interdependent relationship of quality professional learning delivered through the lens of Cultural Proficiency. The result of this design is a clearly stated plan focused on clearly stated student outcomes that embrace the diversity of all learners in our schools.

In Figure 1.1, teachers and administrators who work collaboratively to identify their quality professional learning standards can guide their Culturally Proficient Professional Learning Plan (CPPLP) from the early design stage to the implementation stage using the continuous improvement process. Student assessment data examined through the lens of cultural proficiency allow for continuous monitoring of the CPPLP's outcomes and goals. A prominent feature of this continuous process is benchmarking the formative assessments through the lens of Cultural Proficiency and thereby providing an equitable learning environment. The CPPLP is best designed and implemented through inclusive and collaborative processes.

Collaboration Is Cultural Proficiency in Action

Professional learning is a means to improve educator effectiveness in a way that develops a workplace culture that facilitates the learning of *all* students. Collaborative teams of educators working together can establish appropriate criteria, select complex tasks, and develop numerous approaches that provide diverse students opportunities for authentic responses to multiple assessments and standards-based performance tasks. By coming together to think and plan intentionally and collaboratively, educators and community members can focus on developing an organizational culture that supports career and college readiness inclusive of all students.

The overarching goal of enhancing educational outcomes for all learners means *all* learners. Cultural Proficiency is a mindset for individual and organizational transformation change focused in ways that are inclusive of all students, without exception. When professional learning is designed and implemented using the lens of Cultural Proficiency, participants engage in cultural and academic experiences aligned with professional learning standards and student performance standards. A Culturally Proficient instructor knows and values the importance of standards-based instruction. Embracing student diversity, including all abilities and languages requires teachers to hold high expectations for each and every student. High expectations are implicit in standards-based instruction and hold particular importance in Culturally Proficient educational practices (Voltz et al., 2010).

[handwritten margin note: not Pobreato Syndrome]

MINDFUL USE OF THE
TOOLS OF CULTURAL PROFICIENCY

Schools, as systems, are about communication flowing throughout the organizations. Successful educators communicate well with their students, their students' families, and their colleagues. Effective educators think deeply about their practice both during and after lesson implementation. They share and describe successes and challenges with colleagues using protocols to deepen their learning. Effective educators communicate about educational topics framed by access and equity using those same communication skills and protocols, namely reflection and dialogue. Let's take a closer look at the power and potential of reflection and dialogue as skills for professional learning and ensuring equity and access for all learners.

Power of Reflection and Dialogue

The Tools of Cultural Proficiency provide both the individual educator and the school system a framework and hands-on means for educating all children and youth to high levels of attainment. The journey to Cultural Proficiency begins in effective communication with self and with colleagues.

Culturally Proficient educators engage in personal reflection on their practice as well as become involved in dialogue with colleagues, students, and parents/guardians about shared educational and community interests. In our work with school districts across the United States and Canada, we learned that people and organizations who are effective in cross-cultural communication regularly engage in "thinking about their own thinking" and in "seeking to understand others"—two skills basic to Cultural Proficiency's "inside-out" approach to individual and organizational change.

Take a few minutes to think and respond to the following questions:

- What was your initial response to the phrase—*personal reflection on practice?*
- What was your initial response to *cross-cultural dialogue with colleagues, students, and parents/guardians?*
- To what degree are you involved with your colleagues in conversations about educating all learners?
- What are some ways in which you are engaged in thinking about your own learning (Lindsey, Kearney, Estrada, Terrell, & Lindsey, 2015)?

Please use the space below to record your thinking.

Reflection

_____

_____

_____

_____

When used in mindful and consistent ways, reflection and dialogue are indispensable communication devices that support effective use of the Tools of Cultural Proficiency. Schools are complex organizations composed of countless formal and informal communications networks. Our experience is that when educators intentionally and purposefully use reflection and dialogue, they contribute to healthy school environments for themselves and their students. The intersection of reflection and dialogue with Cultural Proficiency provides benefits:

- For individuals, the Tools of Cultural Proficiency guide reflection to recognize and understand barriers that impede your and your students' learning as well as help develop core values that support and facilitate learning. Once barriers are evident to educators, continued reflective practice drives the use of your cultural assets and your students' cultural assets to sustain learning.

- For groups composed of any combination of teachers, administrators, counselors, trustee/board members, or any persons interested in educational issues, the Tools of Cultural Proficiency provide the opportunity for dialogue to lead to understanding individual and organizational cultures in the school. Similar to reflection, dialogue allows groups to recognize barriers to their and their students' learning and to purposefully embrace the core value that views culture as an asset, and not as a deficit (Lindsey et al., 2015).

The focus of the change process is on shifting thinking and changing conversations from viewing culture as a deficiency to viewing culture as an asset. Intentional and purposeful combination of personal reflection and organizational dialogue leads to the healthy process of an "inside-out" approach to change.

Reflection and Dialogue Foster "Inside-Out" Change

Individual or organizational Culturally Proficient practices are developed through intentional willingness to examine our own behavior and values as well as our school's (or district/board's) policies and practices. Delving into these realms is facilitated through the use of two communication devices referenced above—personal reflection and dialogue. Now that you have thought about and recorded your reaction to these two terms, let's take a look at how we believe these two communication techniques support your learning.

- *Reflection*—the conversation we have with ourselves that leads to even deeper understanding of our own values and beliefs. Sustained reflection often entails exploration of the cultural bases for one's belief systems and for "why" we do the things we do.
- *Dialogue*—the conversation we have with others to understand their values and beliefs. The emphasis is on "understanding" others and not on making decisions, or solving problems, or trying to convince others of the errors of their ways. Dialogue that explores organizational or institutional understanding seeks to explore the bases for stated policies and prevalent practices. Exploration into organizational policies and practices almost always results in the explanation given for current policies and practices: "well, it's always the way we have done it here." True, sustained dialogue seeks to go deeper to understand and explore the historical and/or cultural bases for policies and practices. The deeper dialogue helps members of the organization bring to light deeply held assumptions that have guided decisions and historically determined distribution of resources. Without exposing these assumptions, status quo continues without question or exposure. The questions, "Are we who we say we are?" and "Why do we do what we do?" are the questions that most often help surface long-held assumptions (Lindsey et al., 2015).

Educators using the communication skills of reflection and dialogue to learn and apply the Tools of Cultural Proficiency are well positioned to provide effective, high-level educational opportunities and outcomes for historically marginalized students. Skillful use of the Tools of Cultural Proficiency enable you to intentionally change your practices and the policies and practices of your school in ways that better serve the educational needs of your diverse communities in the context of serving all students in improved ways.

Learning Communities as Collaboration-in-Action: Disturbing the System

Being in or with a learning community does not necessarily guarantee improved student success. Culturally Proficient practices support members of the learning community examining their own values and beliefs and the policies and practices of their organizations regarding how we interact with our students, their families, and their communities. Numerous examples and opportunities for "communities" are found in today's schools. Educators are invited, encouraged, and assigned to work in traditional groups or teams, such as department teams, grade-level teams, faculty study groups, and school leadership teams, including more recent venues such as small learning communities, houses, families, and Professional Learning Communities (PLCs).

Table 1.1 serves as a framework for understanding, analyzing, and sustaining Culturally Proficient Learning Communities.

Table 1.1   A Framework for Understanding, Analyzing, and Sustaining Culturally Proficient Learning Communities

Essential Elements of Culturally Proficient Professional Learning	Elements of Learning Communities	Cultural Competence Characterized by
Assess culture: *Extent to which professional learning addresses cultural identity* Professional learning informs learners about their culture, the cultures of others, and the school's culture. Educational gaps are closed through appropriate uses of cultural, linguistic, learning, and communication styles	Shared personal practice: Community members give and receive feedback that supports their individual improvement as well as that of the organization	• Conducting individual and group assessments • Developing peer-to-peer support toward specific goals • Planning and facilitating intentional professional learning to improve student learning
Value diversity: *Extent to which professional learning addresses cultural issues* Professional learning recognizes and meets the needs of multiple cultural, linguistic, learning, and communication styles	Shared beliefs, values, and vision: Community members consistently focus on students' learning, which is strengthened by the community's learning	• Acknowledging multiple perspectives • Acknowledging common purpose(s) • Basing vision and actions on common assessment results
Manage the dynamics of diversity: *Extent to which professional learning promotes and models the use of inquiry and dialogue related to multiple perspectives*	Shared and supportive leadership (collaboration): Administrators and community members hold shared power and authority for making decisions	• Openly fostering discussions about race, gender, sexual orientation, socioeconomics, and faith as related to the needs of the community

Essential Elements of Culturally Proficient Professional Learning	Elements of Learning Communities	Cultural Competence Characterized by
Professional learning opportunities incorporate multiple perspectives on relevant topics and build capacity for dialogue about conflict related to differences and diversity		• Making decision-making processes transparent and subject to change based on community needs
Adapt to diversity: *Extent to which professional learning facilitates change to meet the needs of the community* Professional learning opportunities use data to drive change to better meet the needs of a diverse community	Supportive and shared conditions: *Structural factors* provide time, facility, resources, and policies to support collaboration *Relational factors* support the community's human and interpersonal development, openness, truth telling, and attitudes of respect and care among the members	• Teaching appropriate communication skills to allow for multiple voices and experiences • Developing adaptive practices to support newcomers as well as veteran community members
Institutionalize cultural knowledge: *Extent to which professional learning shapes policies and practices that meet the needs of a diverse community* Professional learning opportunities are encouraged, shared, and applied in classrooms, throughout the school and the community for the purpose of improving student learning	Collective learning and generative knowledge: Community focus is on what the community determines to learn and how they will learn it in order to address students' learning needs	• Identifying and addressing student needs by benchmarking success indicators • Developing a continuous improvement inquiry model to assess progress toward clearly stated achievement goals

Source: Culturally Proficient Inquiry: A Lens for Identifying and Examining Educational Gaps (Lindsey, Graham, & Westphal, 2008), and *Leading Professional Learning Communities* (Hord & Sommers, 2008).

As you examine Table 1.1, please assume a holistic view of the framework. The Essential Elements of Cultural Proficiency and the tenets of Professional Learning Communities do not exist in isolation from the other elements and tenets. We aligned the approaches,

Cultural Proficiency, and learning communities as illustrations of how school leaders might integrate the elements and tenets. The linear nature of the first two columns of the table does not reflect the dynamics and interactions in which communities engage. Therefore, we added column three to give guidance to communities as they explore opportunities to use the Essential Elements within the context of learning communities. This framework is used to guide learning communities through the lens of Cultural Proficiency.

In reviewing Table 1.1, what opportunities can you find for using the Essential Elements of Cultural Proficiency to enhance and deepen your professional community's learning? Use the space below to record your thinking.

We propose that community members who are willing to closely examine their own thinking, assumptions, and behaviors will disturb their current environments by using the inside-out approach for Culturally Proficient practices to impact and significantly change student achievement, teacher performance, administrator and parent commitments, and school community involvement and support. We suggest opportunities and examples for inside-out disturbances that are immediately within our reach.

- **Classrooms**: Individual educators are more mindful of their own values, beliefs, and behaviors. Educators pay attention to student-to-student interactions, their interactions with fellow educators, as well as their reactions to students and colleagues. Examples include the extent to which educators recognize their gaps in cultural knowledge, their reactions to student and colleague behaviors that may be cultural in nature, and the extent to which they and fellow educators are knowledgeable about the students' neighborhoods in order to develop instructional examples familiar to students.
- **Workrooms**: The ability for educators to examine collective values, beliefs, collective optimism/efficacy, and behaviors.

Examples include the extent to which non-formal conversation centers on the students and their parents/guardians and is reflected in language that views students and parents/guardians as opportunities for educators' cultural learning as opposed to using language that views students and parents/guardians as being the source of problems.

- **Leadership Meetings**: The opportunity for administrators and teacher leaders to demonstrate values, beliefs, and behaviors. Examples include the manner in which culture, both in terms of the school's organizational culture as well as the students' culture, is a normal component of regular meetings, including professional development.

- **Boardrooms**: An on going examination of district and school site policies and practices, involving all stakeholders, to ensure that district and school site policies are responsive to the needs of the diversity of the community. This oversight is particularly important for schools and districts undergoing demographic shifts. Often, shifts in student demographic populations create emergent, new adult responses that prior to the enrollment changes were "invisible." It is incumbent on policy makers to demonstrate decision-making practices that align resources and services with emergent community demographics and student needs.

Each of the illustrations above represents a unique, yet familiar, context for examining and understanding ourselves as individual educators and as members of highly complex schools, school teams, and school districts. Topics of equity, social justice, diversity, and access have historical contexts that are important for us to know in order to understand the value of culturally proficient practices. Later in the chapter, we provide you with a context for understanding the manner in which educational equity has been an unfolding reality in our U.S. and Canadian democracies. We describe how the Tools of Cultural Proficiency are used to deepen understanding of the rationale for Culturally Proficient practices in our schools.

A Shift in Thinking: Both-And, Not Either-Or

Though arguments continue regarding the relevance or efficacy of the No Child Left Behind Act (NCLB) and new college and career readiness standards, our position is how to make the best use of these initiatives in order to narrow and close access and achievement gaps. In the context of the mindless and negative pressures placed on schools and communities for high-stakes testing, NCLB did have a silver lining. It made our profession and nation fully aware of the achievement gap. Amid the mindless testing unleashed by NCLB, the mindset for the initiative was *satisfying high school exit criteria.* The mandate required schools and districts to publish test results by demographic groups, thus exposing what seemed to be the first awareness of the achievement gap. The concept and implementation of college and career readiness standards requires a shift in thinking from the past fifteen years, while preserving a significant achievement of focus on achievement disparities afforded by No Child Left Behind. Including college and career readiness standards for all students and continuing to pay attention to disaggregating student achievement data by demographic groups gives educators the opportunity for "both-and" rather than "either-or" thinking.

The use of disaggregated data is an additional significant opportunity provided by NCLB to be maintained as we move forward with college and career readiness standards. College and career readiness standards bring a focus on the thinking and performance skills necessary for all students to have access to a curriculum that prepares them for college and their career path. Today's educators must think and plan broader than the minimum competencies mandated by NCLB. College and career readiness standards require a redesign and recalibration of the academic environment to provide access for higher order, critical thinking for all learners. In other words, college and career readiness standards can provide leverage to doing what we do best—teaching our students to think and do.

Question *Why?* in Addition to *How?* and *When?*

The legacy of current educational reform movements, if nothing else, may have taught us *how* to do things and *when* to do them. The mantras of educational reform have led teachers knowing *how* to construct various forms of lesson plans, administrators knowing *how* to look for the seven steps in an "effective lesson plan," and both knowing *when* testing is to occur. Leaders must recognize that fellow educators, like their students, are not transposable beings who prosper and grow when fed a diet of reductionist sets of how-to activities. Author Simon Sinek (2009) indicates posing *why* questions leads to effective actions being taken by leaders and their colleagues.

Planning for change that involves diversity, equity, and access, a most important role for the *how* and *when* questions, is made more meaningful by posing the morally laden *why* questions. Cultural Proficiency is an inside-out process of change that values *why* questions.

CULTURAL PROFICIENCY: CONTEXT AND CONDITIONS FOR PROFESSIONAL LEARNING

Throughout this chapter we describe the importance of the relationship of the lens of Cultural Proficiency with Learning Forward's Outcome Standard. We also describe the importance of using reflection and dialogue as strategies for enhancing learning experiences. Now that you have refreshed your knowledge about the power and applicability of reflection and dialogue, you can use this chapter to learn the Tools of Cultural Proficiency and to think how they might apply to your and your school's learning. As you proceed with this chapter you should be able to

- describe Barriers to Cultural Proficiency you may have experienced or observed that limited educator, student, and community member equitable access in growing and evolving in the school community;
- describe how the Guiding Principles of Cultural Proficiency serve as core values to inform your personal and professional learning;
- describe harmful and constructive values and behaviors and school policies and practices and locate them along the Cultural Proficiency Continuum; and
- describe and use the five Essential Elements of Cultural Competence as standards for your personal and professional learning.

The Conceptual Framework as Guide

The Conceptual Framework for Culturally Proficient Practices is presented in Table 1.2. Begin your reading at the bottom of the

Table 1.2   The Conceptual Framework for Culturally Proficient Practices

The Five Essential Elements of Cultural Competence

Serve as standards for personal and professional values and behaviors, as well as organizational policies and practices:

- Assessing cultural knowledge
- Valuing diversity
- Managing the dynamics of difference
- Adapting to diversity
- Institutionalizing cultural knowledge

The Cultural Proficiency Continuum portrays people and organizations who possess the knowledge, skills, and moral bearing to distinguish among healthy and unhealthy practices as represented by different worldviews:

Unhealthy Practices: Differing Worldviews   *Healthy Practices:*

- Cultural destructiveness
- Cultural incapacity
- Cultural blindness

- Cultural precompetence
- Cultural competence
- Cultural proficiency

Resolving the tension to do what is socially just within our diverse society leads people and organizations to view selves in terms of Unhealthy and Healthy.

Barriers to Cultural Proficiency	E t h i c a l	**Guiding Principles of Cultural Proficiency**
Serve as personal, professional, and institutional impediments to moral and just service to a diverse society by		*Provide a moral framework for conducting one's self and organization in an ethical fashion by believing the following:*
		• Culture is a predominant force in society.
• being resistant to change,	T e n s i o n	• People are served in varying degrees by the dominant culture. • People have individual and group identities. • Diversity within cultures is vast and significant. • Each cultural group has unique cultural needs.
• being unaware of the need to adapt,		
• not acknowledging systemic oppression, and		• The best of both worlds enhances the capacity of all.
• benefiting from a sense of privilege and entitlement.		• The family, as defined by each culture, is the primary system of support in the education of children.
		• School systems must recognize that marginalized populations have to be at least bicultural and that this status creates a distinct set of issues to which the system must be equipped to respond.
		• Inherent in cross-cultural interactions are dynamics that must be acknowledged, adjusted to, and accepted.

Source: Lindsey, R. B., Nuri Robins, K., & Terrell, R. D. (2009).

table and follow the arrows to the top of the table. Observe that markedly contrasting sets of values guide behavior. Take particular note of the manner in which barriers are unhealthy while guiding principles as core values inform healthy practices. Recognizing and understanding the tension that exists for people and schools in terms of barriers versus. assets is a good first step in this journey of continuous improvement. Acknowledging barriers that exist for our students and being able to see their cultures as asset-based prepares you for serving the diversity of students in your classroom, school, and district. Take time to read each layer of the table and note how the arrows indicate relationships and patterns of influence.

Barriers Versus Cultural Assets: A Paradigmatic Shift in Thinking and Behaving

The Barriers to Cultural Proficiency and the Guiding Principles of Cultural Proficiency are the "invisible guiding hands" of the framework. Barriers inform the harmful aspects of the Continuum—Cultural Destructiveness, Incapacity, and Blindness—while the Guiding Principles function as core values to guide the constructive aspects of the Continuum—Precompetence, Competence, and Proficiency. Recognizing and acknowledging the Barriers to Cultural Proficiency is basic to overcoming resistance to change within us and in our schools. The barriers to Culturally Proficient attitudes, behaviors, policies, and practices are systemic forces that affect our daily lives and impact professional learning by embracing deficit conceptions of our students and their cultures (Cross, 1989; Lindsey, Nuri Robins, & Terrell, 1999, 2003, 2009). Forces that serve as systemic barriers are the following:

- Being resistant to change and believing that since the current system works for most students, there must be a deficiency with those who can't keep up.
- Being unaware of the need to adapt and expecting that it is those who are not currently successful who are failing to adapt. It can also be that community demography has changed and we continue practices once successful, but not with this community so there must be something amiss with them.
- Not acknowledging systemic oppression by either being oblivious to forces, such as racism or sexism, or dismissing them as artifacts of bygone eras.

- Benefiting from a sense of privilege and entitlement thus well served by current policies and practices and either not being able to see that some communities are served poorly or summarily ignoring discrepant results in the school.

Take a moment and refer back to Table 1.2, noticing the line between the Barriers and the Guiding Principles. That zone or gulf between Cultural Blindness and Cultural Precompetence represents the paradigmatic shifting point where educators have clearly described choices:

- To the left of the line, educators are victims of social forces and embrace a cultural deficit approach to marginalized and historically underserved communities or, every bit as damaging, they regard racism, sexism, ethnocentrism, and heterosexism as societal issues too ingrained for schools to overcome. In contrast, to the right of the line educators choose to believe in their capacity to effectively educate all students, irrespective of their racial, ethnic, gender, socioeconomic, sexual identity, special needs, or faith communities.

The Guiding Principles of Cultural Proficiency are core values that regard students' cultures as assets. The Guiding Principles help identify and overcome both overt barriers that serve to marginalize students as well as the unrecognized and unintentional barriers that serve to limit students' access and eventual academic success. The issue of intentionality is very important; to students, their families, and members of their community overt and unintentional barriers feel the same whether they are intentional or unintentional on the part of educators and the school. Being marginalized sucks!

Culture embraced as asset serves to make the Guiding Principles inclusive. In order to be effective and manifest an inclusive approach to culture, your core values and the school's core values must be deeply held beliefs and values fully vetted by you and members of your learning community. They cannot and must not be lightly agreed to in nodding assent, and then carelessly disregarded. Take a few moments and read the Guiding Principles:

- Culture is a predominant force in people's and school's lives.
- People are served in varying degrees by the dominant culture.

- People have group identities and individual identities.
- Diversity within cultures is vast and significant.
- Each cultural group has unique cultural needs.
- The best of both worlds enhances the capacity of all.
- The family, as defined by each culture, is the primary system of support in the education of children.
- School systems must recognize that marginalized populations have to be at least bicultural and that this status creates a unique set of issues to which the system must be equipped to respond.
- Inherent in cross-cultural interactions are dynamics that must be acknowledged, adjusted to, and accepted.

Please notice that the Guiding Principles are brief, direct, and uncomplicated statements. As you continue your cultural proficiency journey, you may or may not craft your core values with the exact same words as in the Guiding Principles. What is important is to have core values that serve as the moral center of your work and your school's work, because it is our core values that shape our actions. The Guiding Principles inform our actions through the stages of Cultural Precompetence, Cultural Competence, and Cultural Proficiency. It is the alignment of what we profess to value with our actions, both as an educator and as a school, that becomes our outcome measurement. Members of our community can only assess what we do, not what we say.

Transforming the Culture of School

In considering issues of diversity, equity, and access, it is the organizational culture that must be the focus of professional learning. Organizational and school cultures have been studied extensively and researchers concur that schools need leaders who understand and manage that culture in a constructive manner (Deal & Kennedy, 1982; Fullan, 2003; Schein, 1992, 2010; Wagner et al., 2006). Experienced and new educators agree that change is not easy. Implementing new practices in schools is often difficult and made even more challenging when addressing the educational needs of historically underserved or marginalized students. NCLB and similar state-level initiatives have contributed to a slowly evolving national context of responding to the educational needs of marginalized communities in ways not previously confronted. While it may be true that change is not easy, we know also that change in our increasingly diverse society is inevitable and natural.

Formal and non-formal school leaders must be able to recognize and acknowledge personal and institutional barriers to creating conditions for teaching and learning while advocating for practices that benefit all students, schools, and districts. The Conceptual Framework of Cultural Proficiency is a mental model for managing change that we use to understand and tell our stories in ways that may inform as you continue your journey to increased effectiveness as an educator (Dilts, 1990, 1994; Lindsey et al., 2009; Senge et al., 2000).

Cultural Proficiency Holds Cultures to Be Assets

With this basic grounding in acknowledging barriers and using core values informed by the Guiding Principles, we are now prepared to get to the *doing*. The Cultural Proficiency Continuum and Essential Elements of Cultural Proficiency are the most visible Tools of Cultural Proficiency and are represented by what we do, not by what we say we do. The Essential Elements are standards for personal and professional behavior as well as for organizational policies and practices. As noted above, the Guiding Principles are core values that inform and guide the Essential Elements. When culture is embraced as an asset, professional learning goals can be crafted for ourselves as educators and for the communities we serve. Tables 1.3 and 1.4 describe in greater detail the phases of the Cultural Proficiency Continuum and the Essential Elements of Cultural Competence.

In Table 1.3, The Cultural Proficiency Continuum—Depicting Unhealthy and Healthy Practices aligns the six phases of Cultural Proficiency so you can see clearly that the effects of the Barriers are in contrast to the effects of the Guiding Principles. The Cultural Destructiveness, Incapacity, and Blindness phases are composed of harmful behaviors that explicitly or implicitly foster actions that limit the academic and social success of historically marginalized students or the effective exclusion of historically marginalized colleagues and community members. In marked contrast, the Culturally Precompetent, Competent, and Proficient phases are inclusive and support policies and practices for students, educators, and parents/ community members by esteeming their cultures.

Table 1.3   The Cultural Proficiency Continuum—Depicting Unhealthy and Healthy Practices

Cultural Destructiveness	*Cultural Blindness*	*Cultural Competence*	
Cultural Incapacity	*Cultural Precompetence*	*Cultural Proficiency*	

Compliance-Based Tolerance for Diversity	*Transformation for Equity*
• **Cultural Destructiveness**—Seeking to eliminate references to the culture of "others" in all aspects of the school and in relationship with their communities. • **Cultural Incapacity**—Trivializing "other" communities and seeking to make them appear to be wrong. • **Cultural Blindness**—Pretending not to see or acknowledge the status and culture of marginalized communities and choosing to ignore the experiences of such groups within the school and community.	• **Cultural Precompetence**—Increasingly aware of what you and the school don't know about working with marginalized communities. It is at this key level of development that you and the school can move in a positive, constructive direction or you can vacillate, stop, and possibly regress. • **Cultural Competence**—Manifesting your personal values and behaviors and the school's policies and practices in a manner that is inclusive with marginalized cultures and communities that are new or different from you and the school. • **Cultural Proficiency**—Advocating for lifelong learning in order to be increasingly effective in serving the educational needs of the cultural groups served by the school. Holding the vision that you and the school are instruments for creating a socially just democracy.

Source: Adapted from Raymond D. Terrell and Randall B. Lindsey. (2009). *Culturally proficient leadership: The personal journey begins within.* Thousand Oaks, CA: Corwin.

Table 1.4 displays The Essential Elements for Culturally Proficient Practices. This is where doing—the action verbs—are located. Consideration of these five standards without a deep understanding of the Barriers and Guiding Principles rarely leads to effectiveness. The standards are not a checklist, but are carefully crafted standards borne out of a deeply held value for culture in all its manifestations. Engaging in effective professional learning experiences that honor and recognize diverse communities combined with the view that our students' cultures are assets on which to build a relationship better equips us to meet the academic and social needs of historically marginalized students. Take a moment and study Table 1.4, The Essential Elements for Culturally Proficient Practices, and ask in what ways these "actions" can inform your professional learning.

Table 1.4   The Essential Elements for Culturally Proficient Practices

- **Assessing Cultural Knowledge**—Becoming aware of and knowing the diverse communities within your school; knowing how educators and the school as a whole react to marginalized communities and learning how to be effective in serving these communities. Leading and learning about the school and its grade levels and departments as cultural entities in responding to the educational needs of the underserved communities.

- **Valuing Diversity**—Creating informal and formal decision-making groups inclusive of parents/guardians and community members whose viewpoints and experiences are different from yours and the dominant group at the school, which will enrich conversations, decision making, and problem solving.

- **Managing the Dynamics of Difference**—Modeling problem-solving and conflict resolution strategies as a natural and normal process within the culture of the schools and the diverse contexts of the communities of your school.

- **Adapting to Diversity**—Learning about underserved cultural groups different from your own and the ability to use others' experiences and backgrounds in all school settings.

- **Institutionalizing Cultural Knowledge**—Making learning about underserved cultural groups and their experiences and perspectives an integral part of the school's professional development.

Source: Adapted from Raymond D. Terrell and Randall B. Lindsey. (2009). *Culturally proficient leadership: The personal journey begins within.* Thousand Oaks, CA: Corwin.

Being equipped with deeply held values that value culture and diversity through commitment to the Essential Elements as standards prepares one to manage change effectively. Given the complexity of school systems and the diversity of our communities, ensure that many levels are provided to engage organizational change. Where one enters the system to initiate change is important.

Commitment to Improvement— It's the *Why* Question, Again

The change initiative that a school or district holds is often the primary indicator of success or failure in reaching their student performance goals. Level of commitment is reflected in the educators' public pronouncements; the allocation of resources (i.e., inclusive of time, people, money, materials) assigned to the initiative; their widely held beliefs that the initiative can produce desired results; the overall efforts to sustain growth over time; and the ability of teachers and leaders to identify change initiatives as part of *the way we do things around here*. Robert Garmston and Bruce Wellman expanded the work of Gregory Bateson and Robert Dilts by developing a model of intervention based on *the nested levels of learning* (Garmston & Wellman, 1999). Table 1.5 portrays the "nested level" model of behavioral and organizational change that we believe supports consideration and implementation change efforts, such as those in the college and career readiness standards.

Table 1.5 exhibits the Nested Level Change Model, indicating that behavioral and observable changes most significantly occur when all levels are addressed. Change that occurs at one level impacts behaviors below that level (i.e., allocation of resources, decision making, problem solving, professional development, assessment, curriculum, and instruction decisions). Change processes that reside only at the lower levels have little impact or influence on the levels above, limiting the chances or opportunities for large-scale changes (Lindsey et al., 2015).

School improvement efforts focused at the two lowest levels of providing or improving facilities; purchasing materials of instruction; and implementing new academic programs as mandated by local, state, or federal agencies are common in schools and school districts. Such interventions represented as *change* or improvement processes are often employed as *the answer* to problems, such as disproportional suspensions and expulsions of specified cultural

Table 1.5   Nested Levels of Organizational Change

Identity: The individual or group's sense of self

Answers the questions: *Who are we?* or *Who am I?*

> **Belief System: The individual or group's values, beliefs, assumptions, and meanings**
>
> Answers the question: *Why do we do what we do?*
>
> > **Capabilities: The individual and group's reflective and dialogic skills to use new knowledge, understanding, and proficiencies**
> >
> > Answers the question: *How can we develop and use the skills that we have?*
> >
> > > **Behaviors: The individual or group's actions and reactions**
> > >
> > > Answers the question: *What specific behaviors can I or can we employ?*
> > >
> > > > **Environment: Basic physical surroundings, tools, materials, supplies, technology**
> > > >
> > > > Answers the question: *What do we need to begin?*

Source: Adapted from Delores B. Lindsey, Richard S. Martinez, and Randall B. Lindsey. (2007). *Culturally proficient coaching: Supporting educators to create equitable schools.* Thousand Oaks, CA: Corwin.

groups of students. The same answer is often applied to the cultural characteristics of students in advanced placement or honors classes.

Although these lower level interventions are important and necessary, they should be employed after more substantive consideration has been given to answering the *why* question posed by Sinek earlier. Beginning at the lower levels of the change process often becomes "fill-in-the-blank" responses to problems, issues, or needs. New programs or interventions are often seen as the solution to disproportionality or underrepresentation even before student data or student needs are analyzed and appropriate questions posed that challenge operating assumptions. Here are examples of this *fill-in-the-blank* reform model:

- *big brother programs will solve disproportional expulsions and suspensions of students;* or,
- *intense after-school programs will solve the problem for those students.*

Much too often, the *"what"* question is answered before the *"why"* question is asked.

To follow this logic a bit further, we invite you and your colleagues to use this question to guide your professional learning:

- *If _____ is the answer, what was the question?*

Was the question about disproportional student marginalization or regard paid on campus to students' cultures? What data do we have, or do we need, that show the depth of the issue? Did we select the program because of the students' needs reflected in our data? What assumptions were made about historically marginalized groups before data were collected? What other data do we need to gather, disaggregate, and analyze?

Implementation decisions for school change initiatives should be based on student achievement and participation data, involving educators in collaboratively selecting intervention programs, developing instructional techniques, and designing assessment strategies that reflect student needs. Educators have to be engaged in collaborative conversations and data dialogues as part of their district-wide reform efforts to support all students, parents, and community members.

Centrality of Beliefs and Identity

Using Dilts' model (Table 1.5), Cultural Proficiency can be an intervention that occurs at the upper levels of identity and belief systems to ensure equity considerations in implementation of change initiatives that address the academic and social needs of all students. The Tools of Cultural Proficiency guide individuals and organizations to examine their values and behaviors based on their beliefs and assumptions about how students learn and who can learn. This is the *inside-out approach* for changing behaviors and environments. Once an organization's members examine who they are and for whose purpose they exist, they have a greater chance of developing skills and capabilities to address the behaviors and environments within the organization. Once programs are consistent with the organization's identity and beliefs, group members share the responsibility of developing resources in support of those agreed-upon initiatives.

PLANNING FOR PROFESSIONAL LEARNING

Outcomes: Professional learning that increases educator effectiveness and results for all students aligns its outcomes with educator performance and student curriculum standards.

Learning Forward, 2014

Reflection

What does the Outcomes standard mean to you? What is your role in implementing and sustaining an environment where educators can grow professionally and develop students who are prepared for college and career choices? What actions are you willing to take to step forward as a Culturally Proficient leader and proclaim to do something differently to serve educators and their students? We would like you to focus on one particular word in the standard and that word is "all" as in "all students." In the context of reading this chapter, what new learning might you have now that you didn't have prior to your reading? If you didn't experience any new learning, in what ways did this chapter support or inform your thinking? In the spirit of "reflective" practice, we want to give you think time. Take a few minutes and reflect on your own experiences. Write your responses here.

This section provides an integration of the Essential Elements of Cultural Proficiency and the Outcome Standards of Professional Learning (Learning Forward, 2014; Lindsey et al., 2015). At the beginning of this chapter, we presented our framework for understanding and sustaining Culturally Proficient Professional Learning (Table 1.1). The framework displays the Essential Elements for Cultural Proficiency along with the Quality Standards of Professional Learning. The Tools of Cultural Proficiency as an approach for the implementation of professional learning focused on clear student expectations and equitable outcomes for all students. One of the Tools, a set of Guiding Principles, serves as core values for Culturally Proficient Professional Learning.

Educators and their schools who don't manifest deeply held values inclusive of students' cultures may limit their attainment of the goal of narrowing and closing educational access and achievement gaps. Professional learning work is *the work of preparing and supporting educators in ways that ensure all students are well prepared to make choices for college and careers.* Cultural Proficiency can be *the lens* through which you, as an educator, view your work (Lindsey et al., 2009)

- to deepen your thinking;
- to expand your planning; and
- to select actions for using Cultural Proficiency as a lens to design, expand, and examine professional learning.

Professional development/learning involves educators in various structures of Professional Learning Communities for sharing ideas, strategies, visions, practices, resources, and results. In the last generation, education in general, and teaching in particular, has shifted from a compliance model to a standards- and performance-based professional model. More than ever, educators are working collaboratively to design and develop grade- and schoolwide-level assessments, instructional strategies, and appropriate curriculam. These collaborative efforts are intentional and research-based (Hord & Sommers, 2008).

We offer one of Hord and Sommers's key questions: *What should we intentionally learn in order to become more effective in our teaching so that students learn well?* (p. 12). As you consider your personal action learning goals and the action learning goals for your school and district, what is ahead for you? In the section that follows we offer opportunities for you to use the lens of Cultural Proficiency to inform your thinking, your planning, and your actions.

Deepen Your Thinking About Professional Learning

School and education reform initiatives are not new; however, we may be at a turning point of reform (Hargreaves & Fullan, 2012). Our choices may be moving away from *getting tougher on teachers* to a path of co-creating a profession that becomes *more inspiring, tough, and challenging, in itself* (p. 45). The latter choice will emerge from collaborative leadership *that reconciles and integrates external accountability with personal and collective professional responsibility* (p. 45). Sustainable reform and improvement in our profession can be a consequence of educators and teams of educators recognizing and employing the Quality Standards for Professional Learning in a Culturally Proficient manner.

Take a moment and think about Dilts' nested levels for school improvement. Investing in and improving teachers' capabilities through high-quality professional learning that honors and values students' cultures and communities is designed to move all educators in the organization in the direction of improving student achievement for all students in an equitable and inclusive manner.

Professional development and learning is one way to nurture the hearts, minds, and culture of the teaching profession to take the place of antiquated evaluation processes focused on strategies to repair teachers. We offer ways to use the lens of Cultural Proficiency to inform the professional learning of educators and your schools. This process is designed to shift thinking about *all* of our students in an inclusive manner that recognizes and rejects deficit identification in favor of building on the cultural assets of students. The Tools of Cultural Proficiency serve as a lens to apply the professional learning standards as guidelines for becoming the educator you want to be. You are now ready to be mindful in linking planning to action as a Culturally Proficient educator. Once again, we invite you to reflect on your own thoughts and experiences.

Reflection

In what ways has your thinking about professional learning been informed, supported, or shifted from this reading? What new thoughts or questions arise for you as you experience our evolving profession? In thinking about the Outcome Standard, what new insights do you have? Take a few minutes and use the space below to record your ideas, questions, and any "ah-ha" thoughts.

_____

_____

_____

_____

Expand Your Planning for Professional Learning

Effective planning is characterized by being deliberate in such a way that you design and develop a plan with clearly stated outcomes. A thoughtful Culturally Proficient Professional Learning Action Plan (CPPLAP) ensures access and equity by all educators recognizing the influence of the Professional Learning Standards. Shields (2012) describes transformative leaders as inclusive, deeply democratic people who include and engage educators and community members in decision making. Culturally Proficient Learning Plans evolve from carefully documented student needs connected to effective and promising educational practices. The plan is developed, publicized, and thoughtfully implemented. The plan has benchmarks for monitoring data to analyze progress in closing gaps between what was planned and what is accomplished (Fisher, Frey, & Pumpian, 2012). The Culturally Proficient Professional Learning Action Plan as a public guide fosters joint ownership between educators and community members' expectations, goals, and action steps to achieve the goals. Major components of the Culturally Proficient Professional Learning Action Plan are:

- **School Vision and Mission Statements**—The CPPLAP is aligned with your school's shared vision and mission. Community members develop and write the CPPLAP and continuously monitor the alignment of vision and mission statements: Who you profess to be as a school and what is actually revealed by observed behaviors.
- **Current Reality and Rationale**—Planners identify academic and social needs through collecting and analyzing access and achievement data used to guide decisions for establishing desired outcomes and goals. Questions to guide goal setting are: To what extent do current professional learning strategies and structures meet the anticipated needs of curriculum standards? Are additional data needed in order to determine our needs, successes, and challenges?
- **Outcomes and Expectations**—The CPPLAP is designed to inform, develop, and support educators in implementing curriculum standards so that all students are prepared for college and the workforce. Planning teams identify outcomes and expectations that lead to professional learning action steps. Questions to guide desired outcomes, expectations, and

action steps are: Are there reasonable expectations to develop in educators in your school from implementing the Culturally Proficient Professional Learning experiences, knowledge, and skills? What do you want educators to know and be able to do related to the curriculum standards so that all students can achieve at high levels?

- **Goals**—In order to attain desired outcomes for fellow educators and the school, what goals are to be established? In what ways are these goals aligned with the school vision and mission? To what extent are the goals measurable? Setting SMART goals is an effective and efficient process for developing and constructing the CPPLAP. The SMART goal acronym is:

Specific = Responds to questions who, what, when, where, which, why?

Measurable = Develops specific criteria for measuring success by responding to questions such as how much, how many, how will we know?

Attainable = Nurtures knowledge, skills, attitudes, and resources to attain goals through posing the guiding question, what is needed to be successful?

Realistic = Provides perspective by asking whether the goal is high enough and whether we are willing to work hard enough to reach it.

Timely = Develops a specific timeline for benchmarking short- and long-term goals. Measurable goals provide for measuring progress at any point in time, for celebrating points of success, or for identifying areas of needed improvement. Benchmarking is a leadership action to support the teams as they move forward and is based on data rather than on unsustainable assumptions.

Building on the SMART goals and clearly stated Outcomes, Culturally Proficient educators look toward the Five Essential Elements for developing action steps and indicators of success for reaching their goals. The inclusion of community members in the development of these next steps ensures actions toward equity of time, resources, and social capital.

- **Culturally Proficient Action Steps**—Carefully planned behaviors based on best practices and asset-building approaches become action steps for Culturally Proficient educators. Planned action steps use the five Essential Elements for Cultural Proficiency as guideposts. Each of the Elements deepens the professional learning environment through developing a school culture that is comfortable talking about and analyzing issues related to access and equity for the sole purpose of supporting all learners performing at levels higher than ever before. The action steps are pivotal to the success of the CPPLAP.
- **Evaluation and Indicators of Success**—The guiding question for this part of the process becomes—*So, how will we know how we are doing?* That question gives rise to related questions for monitoring the successes and challenges of implementing professional learning plans—*How will you measure success? How often will you measure your progress? What data will you collect?* These benchmarking questions help in measuring progress of actions. Results from analyzing data in an ongoing fashion inform the plan in ways that support continuous learning. Frequent analysis of data allows for revision of the plan as well as continuous improvement of educator practice. Sustaining learning communities toward common standards for all students becomes an outgrowth of continuous monitoring and supporting of plans and demonstrates a moral commitment to democratic education (Lindsey et al., 2015).

Table 1.6, Culturally Proficient Professional Learning Action Plan, supports and informs developing questions about the manner in which schools and districts are inclusive of cultural, demographic groups of students. In what ways can this action plan template support planning for your and your colleagues' professional learning by posing questions about access and equity? In what ways do you and your colleagues use disaggregated data to inform and guide decision making? To what extent do you examine performance or achievement data as a normal part of your planning to determine student academic success by race, gender, language acquisition, or socioeconomic status? At your school or district, is it normative to disaggregate and examine suspension and expulsion data? What needs to occur at the school or district to have such conversations?

Table 1.6   Culturally Proficient Professional Learning Action Plan

Capital City High School

Our School Vision:

Our School Mission:

Current Reality and Rationale: Assessment data *(and other information/observations)*

What are our current professional learning plans and structures for support?

Outcomes: (What is it we want to accomplish for our teachers and leaders? What is it you want educators to know and be able to learn so that all students can achieve at high levels?)

Goal One (*Use SMART criteria*): What goals will we need to establish to reach those outcomes? To what extent are these goals aligned with our vision/mission?

Goal Two

Goal Three

Culturally Proficient Action Steps What actions will we take to reach our goals?	Person(s) responsible (*Positions, not names*)	Resources: Materials and/or personnel	Timeline: When will we benchmark?	Funding:
Assessing cultural knowledge:				
Valuing diversity:				
Managing the dynamics of diversity:				
Adapting to diversity:				
Institutionalizing cultural knowledge:				

Evaluation and Indicators of Success *(toward achieving goal):* How will we measure success? What will we use as benchmarks of success?

SMART Goals:

Specific = Who, what, when, where, which, why?

Measurable = Concrete criteria for measuring success: How much, how many, how will we know?

Attainable = Develop knowledge, skills, attitudes, and resources to attain our goals: What do we need to be successful?

Realistic = Is our goal high enough and are we willing to work hard enough to reach it?

Timely, Tangible = What is our sense of urgency? Can we see it and hear it and feel it and know when we have reached our goal/outcome?

Reflection

Take a few moments to pause and think about what you just read. What new thinking about the importance of developing an Action Plan has occurred for you? In what ways does the Action Plan template inform your work? How do the five Essential Elements enhance the Action Steps for the Professional Learning Plan? In what ways can you use the Elements in your planning? Please use the space provided to take notes that capture your thinking.

_____

_____

_____

_____

Next Step: You Behaving in a Culturally Proficient Manner

As you think about this chapter, we would like to support your thinking through posing a set of questions adapted from Lindsey et al. (2015). We intentionally use the personal pronoun "I" to guide your thinking, planning, and actions:

What is it that I am most intentional about in my teaching and learning?

_____

_____

Who am I, in relation to my colleagues?

_____

_____

Who are we as a professional community?

_____

_____

What am I (are we) learning that will ensure access and equity?

_____

_____

In what ways am I (are we) using what I am (we are) learning about student outcomes?

_____

_____

Who else do we need to include in our community about implementing curriculum standards, and how does that further inform our professional learning?

_____

_____

What (additional) data would be helpful as we develop our Culturally Proficient Professional Learning Plan?

_____

_____

In the closing of the chapter we invite commitment to action steps and dialogic interaction with colleagues. To this point, you refreshed your knowledge of professional learning standards with particular attention to the Outcome Standard and viewed how the standard can be framed with the Tools of Cultural Proficiency. In selecting this book, most likely you already had a commitment to access and equity, and, in that vein, we desire the final words of this chapter to be yours. We pose a set of final questions designed to help focus your future actions and commitment to yourself and your learning community:

- In what ways am I willing to commit myself to use Cultural Proficiency focused on student outcomes as a lens through which I examine and design or redesign my current work?
- In what ways am I willing to commit my learning communities to use Cultural Proficiency as a lens focused on student outcomes through which we examine and design or redesign our current professional learning that focuses on access and equity?
- What are my short- and long-term goals for narrowing access and achievement gaps and outcomes? What will I (we) accomplish with my (our) commitment to this work?
- What are the first steps I take? Second steps? What is my personal Culturally Proficient Professional Learning Action Plan going to be?
- In what ways will parents and members of our communities know of my and our progress toward equitable outcomes for our students?

Use this space to record your responses and your commitments.

_____

_____

_____

_____

_____

_____

_____

_____

_____

_____

_____

_____

Dialogic Activity

Informal conversations and structured dialogue sessions to gain shared understanding of *a school culture in support of all learners performing at levels higher than ever before* is on your horizon. In what ways does the Action Plan (CPPLAP) inform your professional learning? To what extent are you and your colleagues ready to construct your plan? What is currently in place in your school that supports implementation? Continue the dialogue within and among the small learning communities in the school and district. Shared understanding of the school culture related to access and equity is foundational to this plan. What step can you take to fully implement your Action Plan for professional learning in support of all learners, with emphasis on *college and career readiness*?

_____

_____

_____

_____

Stay in Touch

As in all our publications, we want to hear from you. Let us know how things go as you implement your Culturally Proficient Professional Learning Plan. We are part of a community of practice and enjoy engaging with you about your practice and your journey to Cultural Proficiency. Our contact information is

dblindsey@aol.com

randallblindsey@gmail.com

REFERENCES

Armstrong, D. A., Henson, K. T., & Savage, T. V. (2005). *Teaching today: An introduction to education* (7th ed.). Upper Saddle River, NJ: Pearson.

Cross, T. (1989). *Toward a culturally competent system of care.* Washington, DC: Georgetown University Child Development Program, Child and Adolescent Service System Program.

Deal, T., & Kennedy, A. (1982). *Corporate cultures: The rites and rituals of corporate life.* Reading, MA: Addison Wesley.

Dilts, R. (1990). *Changing belief systems with NLP.* Capitola, CA: Meta.

Dilts, R. (1994). *Effective presentation skills.* Capitola, CA: Meta.

Fisher, D., Frey, N., & Pumpian, I. (2012). *How to create a culture of achievement in your school and classroom.* Alexandria, VA: Association of Supervision and Curriculum Development.

Fullan, M. (2003). *The moral imperative of school leadership.* Thousand Oaks, CA: Corwin.

Garmston, R. J., & Wellman, B. M. (1999). *The adaptive school: A sourcebook for developing collaborative groups.* Norwood, MA: Christopher-Gordon.

Hargreaves, A., & Fullan, M. (2012). *Professional capital: Transforming teaching in every school.* New York, NY: Teachers College, Columbia University.

Hord, S. M., & Sommers, W. L. (2008). *Leading professional learning communities: Voices from research and practice.* Thousand Oaks, CA: Corwin.

Learning Forward. (2014). *Standards for professional learning.* Retrieved from http://learningforward.org/standards

Lindsey, D. B., Kearney, K. M., Estrada, D., Terrell, R. D., & Lindsey, R. B. (2015). *A culturally proficient response to the common core: Ensuring equity through professional learning.* Thousand Oaks, CA: Corwin.

Lindsey, D., Martinez, R., & Lindsey, R. (2007). *Culturally proficient coaching: Supporting educators to create equitable schools.* Thousand Oaks, CA: Corwin.

Lindsey, R., Graham, S., & Westphal, R. C. Jr., (2008). *Culturally proficient inquiry: A lens for identifying and examining educational gaps.* Thousand Oaks, CA: Corwin.

Lindsey, R. B., Nuri Robins, K., & Terrell, R. D. (1999). *Cultural proficiency: A manual for school leaders.* Thousand Oaks, CA: Corwin.

Lindsey, R. B., Nuri Robins, K., & Terrell, R. D. (2003). *Cultural proficiency: A manual for school leaders* (2nd ed.). Thousand Oaks, CA: Corwin.

Lindsey, R. B., Nuri Robins, K., & Terrell, R. D. (2009). *Cultural proficiency: A manual for school leaders* (3rd ed.). Thousand Oaks, CA: Corwin.

Ontario Ministry of Education. (2014, April). Achieving excellence: A renewed vision for education. Ontario, Ottawa: Queens Printer. Retrieved from http://www.edu.gov.on.ca/eng/about/excellent.html

Pappano, L. (2010). *Inside school turnarounds: Urgent hopes, unfolding stories.* Cambridge, MA: Harvard Education Press.

Schein, E. H. (1992). *Organizational culture and leadership.* San Francisco, CA: Jossey-Bass.

Schein, E. H. (2010). *Organizational culture and leadership* (4th ed.). San Francisco, CA: John Wiley.

Senge, P. M., McCabe, N., Cambron, H., Lucas, T., Kleiner, A., Dutton, J., & Smith, B. (Eds.). (2000). *Schools that learn: A fifth discipline fieldbook for educators, parents, and everyone who cares about education.* New York, NY: Doubleday.

Shields, C. M. (2010). Transformative leadership: Working for equity in diverse contexts. *Educational Administration Quarterly, 46*(4), 558–589.

Sinek, S. (2009). *Start with why: How great leaders inspire everyone to take action.* New York, NY: Portfolio, Penguin Group.

Slade, S. (2014, June 17). *Classroom culture: It's your decision.* Retrieved from http://inservice.ascd.org/education-resources/classroom-culture-its-your-decision/

Voltz, D. H., Sims, M. J., & Nelson, B. (2010). *Connecting teachers, students and standards: Strategies for success in diverse and inclusive classrooms.* Alexandria, VA: Association for Supervision and Curriculum Development.

Wagner, T., Kegan, R., Lahey, L., Lemons, R. W., Garnier, J., Helsing, D., . . . Rasmussen, H. T. (2006). *Change leadership: A practical guide to transforming our schools.* San Francisco, CA: Jossey-Bass.

Wilmore, E. L. (2002). *Principal leadership: Applying the new educational leadership constituent council (ELCC) standards.* Thousand Oaks, CA: Corwin.

CHAPTER TWO

Beginning at the End

Shirley M. Hord

*A clay pot sitting in the sun will always be a clay pot. It
has to go through the white heat of the furnace to become
porcelain.*

—Mildred Witte Stouven

It is late afternoon in the staff room at rural Hillsdale High School.
Six faculty members, sponsors of the Student Council's fund-
raising drive for their Humanities Project, sit glumly around a work-
table. Five teachers and an assistant principal had been quite
delighted when they were approached by the Student Council about
collecting monies that would impact international nutrition. The
educators were enthusiastic about the students' idea, thinking that
students were turning attention away from their own well-being to
others in need. In addition, this project was not only expanding
student understanding of less fortunate teenagers, but also directing
their focus to an area halfway around the globe that stretched their
geographical perspectives.

A BIT OF A DILEMMA

"What have we done?" asks Dave Eberly, English lit teacher. "We
supported the Student Council in their activities to collect money

that they might contribute to increasing nutrition around the world; I am really pleased that our kids got involved in this project, many of whom live on farms and ranches and have never known what it is to be without nutritious food immediately at hand, and who have never traveled out of the state. But now, one of the parents who provided a significant donation is asking what exactly this is all about, and what specific results we expect will be achieved."

"Well," American history teacher Marilyn Lopez noted, "the project has been a meaningful way to introduce students to the concept of social justice and cultural competence. Actually, subsequent to sending their money, the Student Council learned that each of a number of very small villages in central Africa will receive six guinea fowl, purchased with the funds that were sent. I wonder if they are as puzzled as their parents about exactly what this means. Historically, guinea fowl were indigenous to central Africa, but became almost extinct a couple of decades ago. They are considered a close relative to the pheasant and the meat is considered a delicacy."

"So, what is the game plan and what are the expected results from the presentation of these guinea fowl to a village," Bruce Wiley, economics teacher, inquired. "I am thinking that the provision of the fowl is an action that might lead to a result. Now, what can the results mean, in terms of international nutrition, or a poorly fed village in Africa? Is there a *local goal* that can be achieved at locations around the globe that collectively will add up to international nutrition?"

"If some of the fowl are hens and one a rooster," Dave Eberly mused, "then the village could engage in a guinea fowl production effort that would provide a future supply of fresh meat for the village. Or, on the other hand, if the fowl are all female, the enterprise could be eggs, another continuing source of protein for strong health. But, if they are all male—I don't know about that."

"Ha!" retorted Sam Finch, agriculture teacher, "if two villages would collaborate and if each had fowl of differing gender, the two villages could go into fowl production."

"These are all interesting speculations," Phyllis Bradley, assistant principal, noted. "Perhaps the intention is for the animals to be slaughtered, so there is a feast and enriched nutrition for one evening in the village."

"I think that what we are struggling with is a clear vision of exactly what we would see in a village that received these guinea fowl from a world nutrition organization. What would the outcome of the fund drive look like if it was labeled successful at the village level?"

"You know, it's interesting, but it seems to me that we have a highly similar situation and widespread lack of clarity and clear intention in our school," Bradley continued. "There is a lack of well-articulated goals, results, or outcomes related to the improvement of instructional practices that we want to see in all classrooms. As a result, we are never specifically certain about where we are going, nor what progress we are making, or if we have arrived at our destination—our desired outcome. In a rather bizarre way, this experience with the Student Council has proved to be very enlightening, but it has also provided an important lesson for us—I think. I wonder if there is something here that might be instructive for our entire faculty."

In the Beginning . . .

Since 1994, Learning Forward has given attention, research, discussion, and dissemination to standards that support and promote the quality of educators' professional learning in schools and districts so that every student experiences successful learning. A product of the most recent revision of these standards, the current 2011 standards could be interestingly thought of as sequential. Although all standards are used simultaneously, various ones at particular times require a more intense focus when including the standards in planning and the realization of classroom, school, and/or district changes and improvements. Learning Forward presents the seven standards in this order:

1. Learning Communities—the most significant locale, structure, and strategy for professional learning

2. Leadership—the guide that supports the identified learning and ensures that all requirements for professional learning are given attention

3. Resources—that make it possible for the community members to function and learn well in their community group

   (The three standards above provide the context for professional learning to occur)

4. Data—that are used to initiate the study and make the determination of student and educator needs for learning

5. Learning Designs—provide an array of possibilities for engaging educators in their learning and in the requirements that push such learning

6. Implementation—the process that transfers educators' learning into classroom practice

7. Outcomes—that identify the anticipated educator performance factor(s) and the explicit student learning variables (curricular, social, or behavioral) driving the immediate need for professional learning

There is an implicit order here that is highly congruent with the stages, steps, or strategies of the change/school improvement process. Imagine these seven sequential standards as a cycle with each of them part of the planning and design work for professional learning, and subsequently students' successful learning—and, this cycle is never ending (see Figure 2.1, The Cycle of Learning Forward Standards for Professional Learning).

But where to begin; what is Step One?

The sequence of the Standards in Learning Forward's printed materials begins with the three context-required standards (Learning Communities, Leadership, Resources) that need to be in place so that the learning of the educators can be considered. This means that these standards need initial and continuous attention.

Necessarily, it appears that *action for improvement* begins with examining a wide and rich array of data in order to ascertain where students are performing well and where they are not. Studying data has the attention of those educators who are already data sensitive, and almost always arrests the attention of those who are not so well steeped in the use of data for decision making. Data that reveal low student performance, as well as relevant educator and system data,

Figure 2.1 The Cycle of Learning Forward Standards for Professional Learning

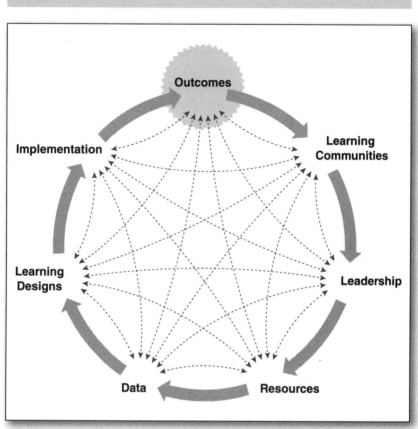

typically focus educators' attention on the low performance and subsequently elicit the following questions:

What should be changed?

What action should we take?

What professional learning do we as educators need?—in order to obtain future data reports whose results will indicate higher levels of performance.

But . . . like a holiday trip, one must know the end point in order to determine where and how to plan and begin. Thus, the articulation of the outcome (shown as the final Standard) is *initially* created in order that each individual involved has a clear statement, vision, and/ or mental image of the result of the professional learning to be provided. This data-based outcome is an imperative and demonstrates the interactivity of the seven Standards. The Data standard is employed as the basis for determining the Outcomes standard by beginning with what is to be achieved. We *begin* with the *end*—which relies also on Resources, Leadership, and Learning Community to support Learning Designs and Implementation to realize the Outcome.

When clarity regarding desired data-based student outcomes has been achieved, and consequently become the focus of educators' professional learning in order to achieve student outcomes, then Learning Designs that define how educators will engage in that learning can be determined. Learning Designs may very well be situated in the Learning Communities whose major purpose is the continuous learning of the professionals. Resources for this learning are provided, and Leadership (including principals, district personnel, instructional coaches, and other teacher leaders) support and assist the professional learners to achieve their learning outcomes. Educators' successful learning leads to their Implementing and transferring their learning into classrooms where it can benefit students. In this way, Outcomes can be achieved successfully.

This brief recitation of a simple scenario to reach Outcomes denies the complexity and needs for intensive planning; not infrequently, years of action may be necessary to realize Outcomes. One might first wonder what and where is the origin or source of these outcomes?

SOURCES OF OUTCOMES

Learning Forward, describing the Outcomes standard, points to two major areas for attention: the performance standards for educators, and the curriculum standards expected of students. Also declared necessary is the coherence of these two bodies of information, and the connection of new knowledge and skills that build on prior learning.

Educator Performance Standards

It would come as no surprise to the public, or to the constituency of any school and/or district, that licensed or certified teaching and administrating staff are on board to serve the community's students. Such licensed staff may not fill all positions in remote or poorly financed schools, but in general, in U.S. schools, educators have been deemed proficient by local, state, or other governmental agencies.

More explicitly, standards for teachers identify what teachers need to know and accomplish to provide an effective, equitable education for every student (Learning Forward, 2011). School and school system leaders (that includes teacher leaders and school or school system administrators) likewise operate under a set of expectations that specifies what these educators should know and execute so that every student and staff member performs at high levels. The work of other members of the educational workforce is guided by definitions of the skills, knowledge, and characteristics needed by those in specialized roles—librarians, guidance counselors, nurses, instructional coaches, and others who serve in critical roles in schools and school systems. All role groups are expected to perform according to the standards—that is, outcomes—defined for their role.

Founder of the professional development organization Research for Better Teaching, Jon Saphier (2011), in his article on outcomes, summarizes the challenge and agreements that high-expertise teaching internationally involves:

> There would be a set of standards universally embraced that clearly defines core agreements about good teaching and learning. . . . Proficiency in the knowledge, skills, and practices that comprise good teaching would be the highest-leverage path to increasing student achievement. . . . Teacher preparation and subsequent professional development for all teachers everywhere would be based on the standards. Every effort would be made to assure that expert practices show up consistently in every classroom. (p. 58)

Student Learning Outcomes

Professional learning for educators must explicitly focus on their work related to student learning outcomes. Further, educators are held responsible for using classroom strategies that will produce the expected and articulated results that identify what students should know and be able to do. When educators' learning is directed explicitly to the outcomes desired of students, Learning Forward reports (2011, pp. 49–50) that this link has a "positive effect on changing educator practice and increasing student achievement." Most assuredly a significant result is realized. Because Learning Forward's language is very clear about this link, it is quoted, "With student learning outcomes as the focus, professional learning . . . can model and engage educators in practices they are expected to implement within their classrooms and workplaces" (p. 50).

Emphasizing the importance of this standard, educator Laura Desimone asserts (2011):

> Professional development that does not increase teachers' content knowledge and knowledge of how students learn content and that is not coherent . . . holds little chance of improving student learning. . . . For example, when teachers do not understand the mistakes children make in their thinking, they cannot correct those mistakes. . . . Many research studies have shown how teacher content knowledge is related to improved teaching and is thus essential for student learning. (p. 66)

School Change and Improvement Outcomes

This set of outcomes may easily be included in the "student learning outcomes" described above. But the frequency and regularity of school improvement projects demand educators' attention to a continuing array of newly identified outcomes for students . . . and, hence, the requirement of educators' learning in order to make the promise of these newly adopted outcomes a reality. Because of the ever-present demands for new professional learning to support changes in newly identified student outcomes, the process that follows describes the adoption and implementation of these particular types of outcomes that are so much a part of the everyday practice of educators and their professional learning.

SEVERAL VITAL UNDERSTANDINGS

The articulation of Outcomes is the initial requirement of the planning and implementation *process* related to a data-informed need for change and improvement in an organization. Regardless of the source that dictates the need for change (see above, Sources of Outcomes), the professional learning that is basic to the change/improvement process of any individual or group rests on the formulation of the outcomes that are desired. Notice the term, *process,* for the identification and successful utilization of Outcomes derives from a process, which we now address.

Perhaps one of the first understandings necessary for considering the successful implementation of outcomes is that any effort to *improve* practice derives from *making a change* from some feature or factor that is not producing desired results to one that holds the potential for doing so; and, to make this change, *learning* is the imperative—learning what the change is and how to use it. This, of course, is what makes Learning Forward and its mission so vital to the continuous pursuit of the ever-increasing quality of any organization—learning is the pathway.

A second vital understanding for school and district organizational improvement is that Learning Forward provides us with the critical elements necessary for high-quality learning; these elements are presented as Standards for Professional Learning, and, as noted above, these Standards appear highly congruent with the research on strategies necessary for successful implementation and change.

And, while these standards target the professionals (that is, educators in schools), the ultimate target of schools and educators is students and their successful learning. Mincing no words, Dr. Stephanie Hirsh, executive director of Learning Forward, unequivocally states, "Student outcomes are the driving force behind professional learning decisions" (Hirsh, 2012, p. 72). Therefore, a third understanding for this discussion is the relationship between adult learning and student learning. (Please review Figure 2.2, The Relationship Between Professional Learning and Student Results.)

This figure makes clear that

- standards-based professional learning (for educators) is a factor that importantly impacts
- educators' changes in knowledge, skills, and dispositions, and that
- these skills and knowledge contribute to changes in educators' practices that
- are transferred into classrooms where (if the change is appropriate) they produce desired changes in student results.

Figure 2.2   Relationship Between Professional Learning and Student Results

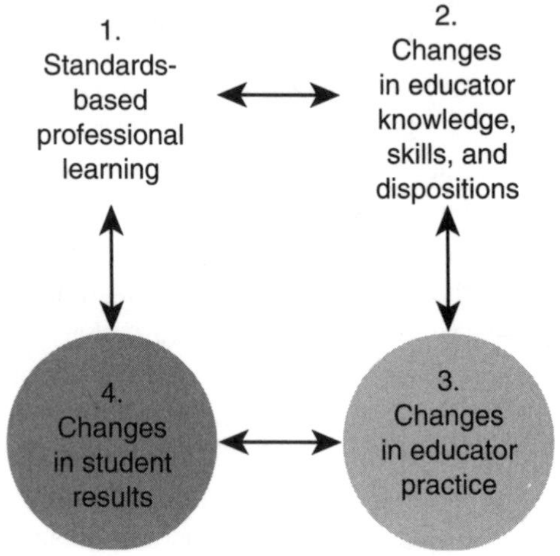

1. When professional learning is standards-based, it has greater potential to change what educators know, are able to do, and believe.

2. When educators' knowledge, skills, and dispositions change, they have a broader repertoire of effective strategies to use to adapt their practices to meet performance expectations and student learning needs.

3. When educator practice improves, students have a greater likelihood of achieving results.

1. Standards-based professional learning ⟷ 2. Changes in educator knowledge, skills, and dispositions

4. Changes in student results ⟷ 3. Changes in educator practice

4. When student results improve, the cycle repeats for continuous improvement.

This cycle works two ways: If educators are not achieving the results they want, they determine what changes in practice are needed and then what knowledge, skills, and dispositions are needed to make the desired changes. They then consider how to apply the standards so that they can engage in the learning needed to strengthen their practice.

Source: Learning Forward (2011).

Professional learning does not directly impact students. As the figure and explanation maintain—*professional learning impacts educators* who influence students. How does professional learning impact educators, and what is the role of Outcomes? The steps of this process are now described.

REALIZING THE RESULTS

Please be aware that the research-based process that describes and explains the journey for successfully reaching desired outcomes of a change effort is challenging and cannot be accomplished in a two-day workshop. But it is eminently doable, and there is a research base that informs us about how to do it. This instructive research derives from studies of the process of change in schools and colleges, and from the literature of adult learning and professional development/professional learning.

Adoption of a Change and Its Outcomes

The first activity of a school or district staff seeking improvement is establishing the need for the identification and development of new outcomes. This group uses the study and interpretation of a broad array of data sources to determine the need for new results. Outcomes are not frivolously plucked from the nether, but their need is clearly perceived as a result of inspecting a rich database of achievement. The initial examination of achievement is that of students, who are the clients and the beneficiaries of educators. Additional data study is given to educators' capacities, knowledge, and skills, and to explorations of the system to determine how these factors impact educators' and students' performance, recognizing that multiple factors influence students' successful learning.

Following the databased identification of student, educator, and system need(s) for change, the next activity is the broad exploration of solutions to the "problem." All too often, this solution selection is not given sufficient time and resources; all too often, a school or district adopts a new practice or program because the school or district in the adjoining neighborhood implemented it. From whatever means, a new practice, program, or process has been identified and is adopted. The activities of exploring data and identifying needs to correct low performance, for example, are followed by study and selection of practice(s) that will correct this undesired circumstance. The activities provided here outline a very brief review of actions required for *adopting* a new practice or program.

Implementation of the Outcome(s)

Attention now is turned to *implementing* the new practice. The first step is clarifying the vision of the new practice—the change—and the outcomes it is expected to achieve. Thus, the articulation of the vision of the outcome becomes the initial and essential focus of attention.

IMPLEMENTATION: ARTICULATING A SHARED VISION OF THE OUTCOME(S)

Please note the word *shared* in the name of this strategy. We live now in an environment of information that is being shared widely by unlimited communication technologies. No longer does the effective "leader" hold information power and use this tool to mandate actions and behaviors of those lower on the power chain. Today, most individuals who care to can arm themselves with information. There is, of course, some amount of confidential material that is not allowed access by the public.

Nonetheless, a first word to the wise for articulating a vision of the Outcomes is to collaborate with others in dialoguing, discussing, and debating aspects or factors of the Outcomes vision—the result of the change effort. Through this interaction (of a group that is neither too small for adequate input, nor so large that useful conversation is prohibited), the group determines firsthand exactly what the expected outcome is and how it will be created. This process gives explicit detailed information about the vision of the outcome so that it can be faithfully used in many steps of the process to reach its realization.

Just as Learning Forward disclosed in a previous publication about Standards (Fullan, Hord, & von Frank, 2015), significant detail about an outcome is required so that participants involved in its implementation understand and can visualize the intended outcome when it is achieved. Over and over, in conducting the research on change in schools, we find teachers and principals interpreting outcomes in multiple ways—when only one way is accurate (Hord & Roussin, 2013, pp. 41–47). This need for precision about the outcome of attention continues to be problematic in any change and improvement effort.

Precision About the Vision of the Outcome(s)

Therefore, the strong suggestion here is to create, as Learning Forward has done, an Innovation Configuration Map (Hall & Hord, 2015), also known as an IC Map. This tool was created to bring clarity to any outcome so that not only written words, but also mental images, are generated for the implementer. These pictures "show" the outcome in operation and show the action (who is doing what) when the outcome is achieved. This "map" also shows the iterations of these actions as novices of the particular outcomes progress from learning about the outcome to becoming skillful implementers of the outcome.

Structures of the
Innovation Configuration Map (IC Map)

Creating an IC Map requires significant amounts of time and energy for its production. Two major structures are used as the format of the Map:

- Components that identify the big or major pieces of the achieved outcome; these components are placed vertically on a chart or table, and
- Variations that describe the component in action; these are placed on a horizontal continuum under its related component.

Please note the example of a simple IC Map that indicates what and how teachers will be using the "New Math" program in classrooms, which reflects the desired outcome of the teachers.

Figure 2.3   IC Map for the New Math Program

IC Map for the New Math Program

Teacher _____

Component 1: Selects Objectives

(1)	(2)	(3)	(4)
Selects objectives, in sequence from the district list, and may add objectives to address the needs of particular students.	Identifies objectives from other published documents that cover the district list.	Refers to other sources for objectives not related to the district list.	

Component 2: Uses Materials

(1)	(2)	(3)	(4)
Uses Heatherton textbook and district supplemental materials, and adds other items to increase student interest and mastery.	Stays strictly within the Heatherton textbook.	Uses other materials collected from teaching experience.	Engages randomly with no systematic set of materials.

(Continued)

(Continued)

Component 3: Engages Students in Learning

(1)	(2)	(3)	(4)
Encourages students to engage in a variety of learning strategies to meet the particular objective and specific students' needs.	Leans heavily on lecture and text assignments, with students self-checking their work.	Maintains careful daily attention to the scope and sequence of the program in order to cover the materials and objectives.	

Component 4: Assesses Progress

(1)	(2)	(3)	(4)
Observes students' daily work, provides weekly tests as benchmarks, and uses district assessments for final evidence of mastery.	Uses the Heatherton text's end-of-chapter tests routinely, and occasionally employs the district mastery test.	Relies on classroom observation of students' work and on teacher-constructed tests.	Employs no regular or systematic assessments.

Component 5: Identifies Next Steps

(1)	(2)	(3)	(4)
Moves students who have mastered current objective to the next objective, and reteaches—using new material—those who have not mastered.	Moves all students along to the next objective in order to cover the program and/or the textbook.		

Source: Hord and Roussin (2013).

Notice that there are five components situated vertically down the page. Notice that each starts with a verb or action word, and when "Teacher" in the upper left of the page is added at the beginning of each component, a complete sentence is made that reveals what the teacher will be doing. In order to reflect the "big" pieces of the outcome, five to eight components are normally sufficient. If fewer are used, then the "pieces" become too large, ungainly, and difficult to think about in their implementation; conversely, if more components are used, they become very "skinny" and tedious because of their larger number. There is no "official" number of components. Good sense and the recognition that the creation ultimately is for understanding should guide the construction of the Map.

Examining the variations of each component, it is obvious that each component does not have the same number of variations. The number of variations is dictated by first establishing the "ideal" variation that can be found in the first, or left, cell of each continuum of variations. Subsequent to identifying the ideal variation, then a series of variations of diminishing value, expected to be found in classrooms (if it is a classroom practice), are established along the continuum with each variation to the right being seen as of lesser value than its immediate predecessor to the left. The number of variations is determined through prediction of what will be found in the site of implementation as the component is implemented. The "site of implementation" is the location, typically classrooms, where the program or practice will be implemented and used.

Creators of the Map

As suggested above, an IC Map is never constructed by an individual. Ideally, the group is small enough so that each participant has sufficient time to contribute reflections, ideas, and suggestions for additions and deletions. But the construction should also include individuals from divergent populations of the expected implementers, some of whom should be positive supporters of the Outcomes implementation and some who have reservations. Certainly, there must be some persons who serve as expert sources for what the components of the outcome should include. And one or more leaders should be sufficiently comfortable with this procedure to support and guide its work.

An initial draft of the Map does not prepare it for use with implementers. The draft should be revisited after several days in order for the designing group to review its work and make corrections. Subsequently, the revised draft should be field-tested with a small number of potential implementers in order to ascertain if the language of its components and variations is understandable and makes sense. If not, further revisions should be made and testing done again.

Introducing the IC Map, the Precision Tool

The revision and completion of the Map is not the end of the story—the Map must be used. This stimulates the challenge of how to engage principals and teachers in understanding the Map and how to use it. One schema for doing this suggests convening the school staff in its regular meeting space. Provide each individual with a copy of a Map. Use Figure 2.3, the New Math Map, as your illustration. Ask individuals to remain silent and to read the Map. Share that the #1 variation describes the desired outcomes of the change effort in which they are being involved. Ask them to close their eyes and visualize in their mind, "What action do they 'see' happening as they read about each component?"

Invite individuals to share their mental image and the cell's text that relates to that image. Remind them that this Map provides the expectations for what the teachers will be doing in their classrooms when using the New Math Program.

In simple terms, the #1 cell describes what the teachers will learn to do and it defines the outcomes of the teachers' study and learning. Reemphasize that the teachers will be learning this new way to teach math, and that their learning precedes the students' learning. There will be a different Map that defines and illustrates the outcomes that the principals will achieve.

Invite teachers' attention to the components and that they represent the large segments of the outcomes that teachers will attain. Direct their attention to the variations of each component and their function and meaning. Support the group in understanding that this Map is a written introduction to the New Math Program; it describes what they will be doing when using the Program, and will be used to set expectations for each successfully implemented component's ideal variation. The Map will be used in other ways that will become clear as implementation develops. At this point, the Map provides clarity about the Outcomes that they will work to achieve.

Conclude this session by acknowledging that much time and effort has been invested in constructing the IC Map, and for good reason. It will guide them and their learning partners as they work to implement the new program and realize the Outcomes associated with their role. IC Maps have been used widely for many different change projects and the professional learning that they require. Stress that many users of the Maps have given positive confirmation of the effectiveness of the Maps and their use. Suggest that this instrument communicates very succinctly about new practices and programs, a factor that they appreciate a great deal.

Much space and text has been given to the description and initial function of the IC Map. The length and detail has been deliberate here in order to develop understanding of the Map and the role it can play in contributing to the articulation of a vision of the change— understanding that this vision represents the Outcomes that are desired for a school and/or district's quest for improvement.

Additional employment of the Map is highlighted in subsequent strategies that support implementation of an improvement effort's outcomes.

IMPLEMENTATION: PLANNING AND IDENTIFYING NECESSARY RESOURCES

Only the foolish embark on a journey without a roadmap for the trip's intended end point. Assuredly, planning and preparation, when done well, contribute to the successful culmination of the journey. Taking such action to achieve educator and student learning outcomes demands no less, since we compare reaching these wished-for results as a journey. Therefore, six research-based strategies (Tobia & Hord, 2002) are explored for their engagement in this journey—the first strategy is titled Articulating a Shared Vision of the Outcome(s), which is thoroughly discussed earlier in this chapter. Having defined the vision of the Outcomes in a precise way through creation of the IC Map makes it possible to meaningfully discuss the remaining five actions necessary for implementation.

The specific written text (the IC Map) and mental images of the Outcomes provide the foundation for the second strategy, Planning and Identifying Necessary Resources. The Map is our guide for creating a plan and giving attention to the resources required for implementation. The Map stimulates attention to multiple factors and questions about resources:

- Is new staffing required, or are existing staff's responsibilities modified, and if so, when and how is this noted in the plan?
- How much time is required in the plan for professional learning and preparing staff for the new practices envisioned, and how much estimated time (across months or years) is needed for staff to become experts in their new roles?
- What equipment and instructional materials need to be supplied, and what is the time frame?
- Does the existing organization's structure of student grade levels and teacher teams need adjustment?
- How do we stay abreast of our change process, what concepts and tools enable us to do this, and when in the plan do we assess progress?
- How do we know if our efforts are successful, and if we are nearing realization of our outcomes?

In any specific setting or context, there are many other questions to address, but these listed above are basic as starters to any change and improvement process. An additional and highly important part of the plan is a consideration and identification of the person or persons who will lead, guide, and support the plan so that it contributes meaningfully to implementation.

IMPLEMENTATION:
INVESTING IN PROFESSIONAL LEARNING

As stated earlier, any improvement, whether it is as disparate as an upgrade to the AC/heating operations in one's domicile or targeting students' creative writing skills, is based on changing a nonproductive feature(s) for some new element that promises better results. And learning is key to that change: learning what the new practice is and how to use it. A review of the components of the Outcomes IC Map informs us of the professional learning that is required for implementers to succeed with each component at the ideal variation; and on our plan, who is privileged to the learning, and when, where, and how it is designed and experienced.

Because adult learning provided to school and district professionals so often has been superficial and ineffective, we are sharing a short review of Joyce and Showers' research on the components revealed as necessary for successful professional learning and its transfer to classrooms where the adult learning benefits students (2002, pp. 78–79). For years, Bruce Joyce and colleagues have studied the effects of professional learning provided to teachers, and the results of this research aid us in designing and conducting learning sessions for adults. These four components and their results (effects on Knowledge attainment, Skill development, Transfer/Implementation to the site where the learning is employed) are:

1. Adults *told about or reading about* a new practice results in no achievement of Transfer/Implementation of the new practice into the classroom.

2. Adding *demonstration or modeling* of the practice results in no gains for Transfer/Implementation.

3. *Practice with feedback* produces a significant increase in Knowledge and Skills, but only five percent success in Transfer into the classroom.

4. A significant difference is gained in all results (Knowledge, Skill, Transfer/Implementation) with the *cumulative use of the first three components and the addition of peer coaching*— the focus of attention by these researchers for multiple years in multiple settings.

Joyce and Calhoun have developed and researched strategies for creating the peer coaching factor for schools, but this is a topic for the Leadership volume of this series of seven books focused on Learning Forward's Standards for Professional Learning (upcoming).

If improvement is based on change, and change is realized through learning, as we have maintained throughout this series of books and as indicated by the Joyce and Showers research report, professional learning is imperative. This imperative underscores the clear need for quality professional learning, achieved through the Learning Forward Standards. The content of this learning includes what the educators need to know and be able to execute in order to realize the desired outcomes of the change project.

Thus, what learning is required by the staff involved in the implementation of the new practice? As suggested above, the IC Map provides guidance for the response to this question. Leaders of change should be acutely aware that the learning is not delivered in a two-day large group learning session (period!), but is provided over time in manageable segments to meet the needs of staff throughout the implementation process. And, there is specific learning that change leaders and facilitators need in order to support the process of implementation with the staff. The specificity of the learning for all role groups can be found in the IC Maps for each role group. This, again, points to the value derived from the Maps.

In addition to the content of professional learning gained from the Maps, and the wisdom elicited from the research of Joyce and Showers that guides us in the process of the learning, Learning Forward now directs our attention to the prerequisites for professional learning (Learning Forward, 2011, p. 15):

- Educators' commitment to *all* students is the foundation of effective professional learning. Educators' continuous learning is directly related to increasing each student's performance. Learning Forward precisely tells us that "If adults responsible for student learning do not continuously seek new learning, it is not only their knowledge, skills, and practices that erode over time. They also become less able to adapt to change, [become] less self-confident, and [become] less able to make a positive difference in the lives of their colleagues and students."
- Each educator involved in professional learning comes to the experience ready to learn. Most of us have witnessed those educators who use professional learning time to make next week's lesson plans, score students' creative writing paragraphs, or work today's crossword puzzle. Fortunately for our students, these individuals are among the modest few in any session and can almost certainly be coaxed into engaging in the learning with their colleagues—but, of course, this requires a bit of time, attention, and clever action on the part of colleagues and/or learning session facilitators.
- Because there are disparate educator experience levels and use of practices, professional learning can foster collaborative inquiry and learning that enhances individual and collective

performance. This puts honesty, transparency, and trust front and center. These characteristics may develop as educators work collaboratively, but in addition may require their creation and development through the support of leaders and facilitators.

- Educators, just like all learners, learn in different ways and at different rates.
- This truth demands differentiated learning designs that address particular learning needs, that require more or less time for the various learners, and that provide a variety of learning styles and experiences. For further examination, always keeping in mind the link of educator learning to student outcomes, we recommend a paper authored by Joyce and Calhoun in the introduction of the Standards in *JSD* (2011, August), which focuses on the Learning Design Standard.

IMPLEMENTATION: CHECKING PROGRESS

One of the major challenges, and sometimes an uncomfortable activity for those guiding a change effort, is to *ensure* that the identified outcome(s) becomes a reality. This means tracking the implementers' learning that was provided in order to achieve the outcomes, and assessing its progress as it moves through the process of implementation. It is at this period that much observation, interactive dialogue with the implementer, and attention must be brought to assess progress toward the desired outcome so that appropriate support can be provided if needed. These activities are critical to successfully achieving the outcomes.

Of course, observing and supporting the process of implementation from the beginning is highly important. But it is critical as implementers begin to use new practices that they are closely followed by their supportive facilitators. It is very unusual for individuals to be completely free of needs for clarification or relearning through modeling and/or demonstrating in the classroom when they are in the early (or even later) stages of transferring their learning into classrooms. These assessment activities may be done by experienced facilitators or by colleagues who have mastered the knowledge and skills, have developed their capacities, and are able to share with others.

All too frequently, change leaders assume that the implementers' learning has been successfully mastered. All too frequently, novice implementers are shy about asking for help. All too frequently, facilitators assume that if implementers do not ask for help, that they do not require help. Thus, there is the imperative for colleagues or facilitators to initiate contact and to establish helping relationships with implementers. Inviting an implementer to have a cup of coffee and chatting "socially" about the change with no critiques included can open the door for the facilitator's follow-up action that is more focused on implementation. No person is left unattended; if individuals do or do not request assistance, facilitators should be extending goodwill, pleasant interaction, and useful support.

What we know is that when anyone is given attention and assessed, they are more likely to accomplish any task. And because change does not occur in a few days or a week, implementation must be continuously monitored using the outcomes as a yardstick to make judgments about progress, which in turn goes back to the integral IC Map that describes the outcome(s).

Many successful leaders and facilitators use the IC Map, as previously reported, to introduce and make certain that implementers have a clear vision of the outcomes to be achieved. The Map is also used to determine the learning demanded of the implementers; it supports facilitators in the careful design and conduct of the learning with those who implement the change in order to realize the outcome(s). But, subsequent to all learning activities, the learning implementers are observed in order to ascertain if their learning accurately results in the transfer of the desired knowledge and skills into classrooms where they can benefit students. Using the Map as a yardstick to measure implementation progress is done successfully by many facilitators. Rather than always observing, many of these supporters sit with the implementer and use the Map to guide collegial conversation about the implementer's current position on the Map. "Collegial" is the operative word here, as facilitators generate a collaborative and mutually respectful relationship with the implementer.

Despite the availability of an IC Map that clarifies the outcome, and though time and abundant resource materials were supplied, and standards-based professional learning was provided, the process of making a change and realizing its outcome is unlikely to be free of surges and stumbles. Keeping the process on track is the work of facilitators who give their attention to *each* implementer as he or she engages in the work of authentically installing the change in classrooms.

Using the term "checking progress" is preferred to monitoring or assessing, for checking progress denotes a positive demeanor, although in many cases, progress may be very slow. Nonetheless, the frequent (weekly or biweekly) facilitator's interaction with the implementer should result in the implementer's feeling of being valued and worthy of support. It is highly predictable that full implementation and attainment of the outcome will never be reached if this regular and systematic check of progress is not maintained. Thus, no matter how large or small the progress to full implementation and results, celebrations should be conducted based on evidence of progress. These celebrations may be done publicly or privately, which is dependent on the prediction of the implementer's appreciation.

In addition to use of the IC Map to trace progress of implementation of the desired outcome, there are additional tools that may be easily used for this purpose. Please review Chapter Two of a 2015 book by Fullan, Hord, and von Frank—one of a series of seven books that focus on each of Learning Forward's Standards for Professional Learning. Their book focuses on the Implementation standard and provides tools that elicit concrete evidence of an implementer's progress (e.g., One-Legged Interviews are described).

Please note: collecting information on the progress of each implementer is a significant waste of time if nothing is done with these data. . . . Now what could that mean?

IMPLEMENTATION: PROVIDING ASSISTANCE

Assistance and Assessing (as noted, the preference is to use "Checking Progress") act like the hand in glove in that the two steps that are requirements for high-quality implementation are inextricably linked—or should be. While checking and collecting data on progress could be the basis for celebrations, the more potent employment of data is for determining support and assistance for the implementer. Where assessing and assisting meet is the point at which the rubber hits the road—to be rather colloquial. As the research of Joyce and Showers (2002) indicates, extensive learning about a change that will produce new outcomes for staff and subsequently for students requires a lengthy process of 1) reading or being told about the "new way," 2) seeing the "new way" demonstrated or modeled, 3) giving many opportunities for practicing the "new way" followed by feedback on the practice, and 4) providing ongoing follow-up by coaches or facilitators.

These steps in the successful learning of new practices and their transfer into classroom use, to achieve designated outcomes, require much time and support. The support may be simple: supplying additional materials; conducting small group re-teaching sessions; making time for one-to-one, face-to-face interactions to clarify issues or solve problems; or most vitally, working supportively to enable the implementer to meet high-quality, outcomes-based implementation. Additionally, these actions by the facilitator are in direct response to the assessment data collected, data that indicate needs. Importantly, if the implementer doesn't request support from the facilitator, the facilitator must not assume that all is well with the implementer. The facilitator must reach out and establish a positive relationship with every implementer so that any shyness about asking for help (or resentment about doing so) is forgotten as the implementer seeks assistance—and doesn't have to seek very long or hard. Therefore, the first activity of the facilitator is simply to stop by each implementer's workplace and extend welcome and a friendly greeting and handshake.

The role of the facilitator cannot be overstated or too frequently reminded of its power and importance to the process of implementing a change of practice that will produce new outcomes. Whether working with an early adopter who is a novice related to the change or working with those who have been engaged with the change for a lengthy amount of time, or whether the implementer is making small steps or giant leaps in the process of achieving new outcomes, the operative word for facilitators is support, support, support.

And, in addition to all of the aforementioned structures and strategies, there is yet another that is necessary for implementation of the outcomes.

IMPLEMENTATION:
CREATING A CONTEXT THAT NURTURES CHANGE

Increasingly, the culture of the workplace is being reported about, given attention, and undergoing rigorous study. The context, climate, or culture—whichever term selected—impacts the staff. Context is the integration of two dimensions: the *physical* elements of the organization, such as its organizational structures, schedules, and policies, as well as its facilities; the second is the *human* factor represented by the organization's personnel and their beliefs and values and the norms that direct their attitudes, behaviors, and relationships. These two dimensions interact and influence each other. This is especially true when change initiatives are introduced.

A school and/or district context that is supportive of its members decreases the isolation of its members. A colleague in an education unit in Australia once commented that the morning bell for tea's real purpose was to encourage the large staff to come together regularly for both "official" and casual conversation.

A supportive environment continues to nurture the staff's capabilities, most especially those related to the new outcomes. The supporting culture fosters positive relationships among staff and between students, parents, and the community. It encourages risk taking so that implementers engage in new behaviors, and it forgives mistakes when learning accrues from the analysis of the mistake. Thoughtful facilitators use tools, such as Stages of Concern (Hord & Roussin, 2013), to identify the reactions and feelings of implementers in order to continuously provide support that is appropriate and effective. And, those in a supportive culture advocate, without ceasing, for continuous change in practice and outcomes so that increased school effectiveness reigns and students benefit.

IMPLEMENTATION: THE CHANGE FACILITATOR

In this chapter, much attention and action have been encouraged in order that newly stated outcomes lead to educators' new practices that lead to improved student performance. New outcomes cannot be produced without significant learning of educators so that change of practices occurs. The attention, action, and educator learning all depend on the knowledge, skills, and helping attributes of the facilitators who guide and support the change effort. Whatever the supporters' official role: principal, assistant principal, lead teacher, department head, grade-level chair, coach, instructional aide, or other assignments, they also wear the facilitator's hat. Their tasks and challenges are not easy, although they may sound simple in the text devoted to the facilitator. However, their work comprises complex undertakings (Hord, Rutherford, Huling, & Hall, 2014); theirs is a highly significant and vital role.

To these heroic persons who perform a highly sensitive and practical role in the implementation of new outcomes in our schools so that all students learn well, we share a note from Ernest Hemingway,

It is good to have an end to the journey toward;

but it is the journey that matters, in the end.

OBJECTIVES? GOALS? RESULTS? OUTCOMES?

In reflecting about our work with educators in the field, it seems that educators' language suggests objectives and goals as statements of intention, or hopes, or expectations for accomplishment. Outcomes and results appear to be statements of what has been achieved . . . and such statements seem stronger and more "picture- or vision inducing."

When my colleagues and I work in the field with educators on their improvement efforts, we typically and initially inquire about the goals that the project is meant to attain. All too frequently, the responses are about actions that will lead to a goal; there appears to be much confusion about goals and actions. Therefore, we ask, what is the result or outcome that you are trying to achieve? This appears to produce a puzzled frown; screwed-up eyes that suggest that thinking is occurring; and a wee smile that acknowledges that there may be more to this matter of objectives, goals, and results or outcomes than they had previously imagined. It seems to put a different slant on the conversation. Language is, of course, an enduring challenge, and selecting the terms that best communicate is always part of this process.

As the quotation at the beginning of this chapter suggests, we will not produce the hoped-for elegant porcelain of our outcomes without first understanding clearly what the outcome(s) are so that this clear understanding drives the "heat" of our actions and events to achieve the outcomes. This essential "heat" is the essence of this chapter.

P.S.
We never learned the specific intention or clear objective of the six guinea fowl . . . an enduring mystery.

REFERENCES

Desimone, L. (2011, August). Outcomes: Content-focused learning improves teacher practice and student results. *JSD, 32*(4), 63, 65–68.

Fullan, M., Hord, S. M., & von Frank, V. (2015). *Reach the highest standards in professional learning: Implementation.* Thousand Oaks, CA: Corwin.

Hall, G. E., & Hord, S. M. (2015). *Implementing change: Patterns, principles, and potholes.* Upper Saddle River, NJ: Pearson.

Hirsh, S. (2012, October). From the director. *JSD, 33*(5), 72.

Hord, S. M., & Roussin, J. L. (2013). *Implementing change through learning: Concerns-based concepts, tools, and strategies for guiding change.* Thousand Oaks, CA: Corwin.

Hord, S. M., Rutherford, W. L., Huling, L., & Hall, G. E. (2014). *Taking charge of change.* Austin, TX: SEDL (Southwest Educational Development Laboratory).

Joyce, B., & Showers, B. (2002). *Student achievement through staff development* (3rd ed.). Alexandria, VA: Association for Supervision and Curriculum Development.

Joyce, B. R., & Calhoun, E. F. (2011, August). Learning designs: Study, learn, design, repeat as necessary. *JSD, 32*(4), 46–47, 49–51, 69.

Learning Forward. (2011). *Standards for professional learning.* Oxford, OH: Author.

Saphier, J. (2011, August). Outcomes: Coaching, teaching standards and feedback mark the teacher's road to mastery. *JSD, 32*(4), 58–59, 61–62.

Tobia, E. F., & Hord, S. M. (2002, March). Making the leap: Leadership, learning, and successful program implementation. *Instructional Leader.* Austin, TX: Elementary Principals and Supervisors Association.

Chapter Three

The Case Study

Valerie von Frank

USING THIS CASE STUDY

Most readers of this case study will find a district that is different from theirs. The temptation is to say this district is too rich or more disadvantaged, larger or smaller, more urban, more rural, more or less diverse. Doing so misses the value of a case study.

The questions at the heart of the matter are about how well this system stands up when we consider the major strands of this specific standard for professional learning. In reading the case study, it's fair to ask how the system meets the individual standard, as well as in what ways it may not. It's helpful to consider how well the district meets the other standards for professional learning, which top-performing systems generally do because of the interconnected nature of the standards. Most effective systems working to achieve one standard strive toward quality professional learning that meets multiple standards. But in the real world, as they reach, they also may fall short in one area or another.

The decision for this series to use real, journalistic-style rather than fictionalized case studies was deliberate. The intent is for readers to hear educators' voices from actual practice, to see examples of what is possible and what it looks like to work to the level of a specific standard for professional learning—including some aspects that may not fully exemplify the standard. The districts were chosen based on research, interviews, and solid evidence that student outcomes are improving, because student achievement is the ultimate goal of professional learning. Professional learning does not take place for its own sake, but to enable teachers to teach effectively so that every student achieves.

Often these days it seems we are tempted to focus on our differences rather than seeking the good we can find in the model before us. Reading a case study should invite that certain amount of critique, but also of recognition if not admiration. Rather than losing the point by focusing on differences and perceived shortcomings, we invite you to consider the standard at hand. Review its main components. Ask how this district exemplifies those elements. Listen carefully to what those at each level of the system said about learning from their vantage point.

Ask probing questions, either as a reader or with colleagues, and use the case as it is meant—for thoughtful discussion of a district's strengths, areas for improvement, and more than as a comparison with your own or an ideal, as a launching point for discussing how the standard for professional learning strengthens educators' core work and makes possible greater student achievement. When you have delved deeply into the standard itself, the next step is to look within your own district to determine how the standard can be used to improve your system.

At the end of the case study, you will find a set of discussion questions to prime your reflection, analysis, and discussion. We encourage you to meet and discuss this district's implementation of professional learning with a few colleagues and share your insights with other school and district staff.

In Miami-Dade County Public Schools, the focus on student learning doesn't mean leaders treat all schools equally. Instead, they focus on equity—making sure schools that need more receive more. And in the nation's fourth largest school district, student outcomes are improving as a result.

Consider the degree to which student achievement has improved:

- Miami-Dade outperformed most large city school districts across the country on the National Assessment of Educational Progress Trial Urban District Assessment, earning higher average scale scores in nearly every category of mathematics, reading, and science for fourth and eighth grades in three testings: 2009, 2011, and 2013.

- The district earned an overall B grade in nine of the last ten years on the statewide accountability report card (2014 results are preliminary). The grades are assigned based on student achievement in the Florida Comprehensive Assessment Test (FCAT) in the four subject areas, as well as student learning gains and the progress of students in the lowest quartile.
- More than half of the district schools earned an A on state report cards in 2014.
- After being named a finalist for the Broad Prize for Urban Education five times, the district received the top national prize in 2012.
- The district's graduate rate is above state averages, an exception for large urban systems. Graduation rates rose five percentage points to 76 percent in 2011–12 from the prior school year.
- In 2014, The College Board named Miami-Dade the Advanced Placement Equity and Excellence District of the Year among large districts for expanding access to Advanced Placement courses while simultaneously improving AP performance (College Board, 2014). In a news release, College Board President David Coleman noted that Miami-Dade provides the evidence that "equity and excellence can be achieved in classrooms across the country."

Miami-Dade, with more Latino and poor students than most districts in the nation, may be the premiere example of how much children in a large, urban system can achieve as the nation's population shifts rapidly toward a majority made up of Latino, African-American, Asian, and other people of color. Public schools hit that milestone in the fall of 2014 (Maxwell, 2014).

Consider what it means to be among the largest school systems in the country.

How large is Miami-Dade Public Schools? The district has

- More than 350,000 students—if the kids formed their own city, that city would just about break into the top fifty list for largest in the nation. The number of students equals the total population of Tampa or Honolulu, Hawaii.

- Nearly 22,000 teachers—more teachers than are employed in any of 14 states (Alaska, Delaware, Hawaii, Idaho, Maine, Montana, Nevada, New Hampshire, North Dakota, Rhode Island, South Dakota, Vermont, West Virginia, or Wyoming) and nearly as many as Nebraska, New Mexico, Oregon or Utah (National Center for Education Statistics, 2014).
- A total of 46,000 staff—just about enough to sell out the seats in Baltimore's Camden Yard, home to the Orioles.
- 340 schools in 2013–14, although the number of operating buildings fluctuates.

How poor are students here? Three of every four enrolled have qualified for free and reduced price lunch.

How diverse is the student body? In addition to Spanish, students' first languages range from Haitian Creole, French, Portuguese, and Zhongwhen (Chinese) to Russian, Arabic, Vietnamese, Urdu, and Italian.

Facing such challenges, many urban districts liken themselves to battleships rather than speedboats—getting turned around takes time. For Miami-Dade, it was less time and more attitude that has students, particularly Hispanic students in the system, outperforming many other urban districts around the country.

The attitude seems to stem from Superintendent Alberto M. Carvalho, a district native who rose to the top job in 2008. When Carvalho was named superintendent, the state was threatening to close nine schools, many that were anchors in parts of the district that were largely African-American.

"We were in the middle of the recession," he says. "Our district was at three levels of bankruptcy: an academic bankruptcy, a financial bankruptcy, and certainly an ethical bankruptcy," Carvalho was quoted as saying (Adams, 2013).

Carvalho set out to solve the issues using "a zero-based, moral-values-based budget" (Rosen, 2011). "We identified what our non-negotiable principles were, and we imposed those principles on the budget discussion," he said (Rosen, 2011).

According to Enid Weisman, chief human capital officer, Carvalho called for massive budget cuts that focused on the administration, putting many administrators back into classrooms and cutting $450 million in the first three years out of a $6.5 billion budget. "We took the fiscal cliff also as an opportunity to really look at practice, efficiencies, student outcomes, explicit teaching, and high yield strategies," she said, and leaders began directing resources to the most "fragile" schools.

"From the beginning, we keyed in on the student outcomes," Weisman said.

For Carvalho, the issue was that simple. "This is imminently doable work," he said (D'Orio, n.d.).

A UNIQUE SYSTEM

Miami is sometimes called the new Ellis Island, because many see Miami International Airport as the nation's gateway to the Caribbean and Latin America. Miami-Dade County has seen double-digit growth over the last two decades, mostly from immigrants. More than seven in ten residents have a first language that is not English. In fact, 51 percent of county residents were born outside of the United States, half of those in Cuba. Cuban refugees began arriving in the city by the thousands in the 1960s. An influx of new residents followed from Nicaragua and Haiti, and then from other central and South American countries where emigrants sought to escape poverty, politics, and violence.

The district is also geographically diverse, covering two thousand square miles and encompassing the Everglades and downtown Miami's skyscapes. Like most large urban districts with significant poverty, Miami-Dade's student results are lower than national average scale scores. Yet, although the state raised its reading and math standards in 2012 and began to include second-year English language learners, and then raised the bar for writing and science in 2013, Miami-Dade can claim about six in ten students reaching at least proficiency in math, reading, writing, and science. The system's most impressive gains are from students in the lowest quartile on performance indicators.

These results may be based on the system's investment in "human capital" through the Office of Professional Development and Evaluation, a department with four branches: professional development, teacher growth, leadership development, and performance

Miami-Dade's student enrollment is 355,268. The student population is 68 percent Hispanic, 23 percent African-American, 8 percent white, 1 percent Asian, and 1 percent other (totals are rounded). Economically disadvantaged students form 73 percent of the student population, and 26 percent of students are English language learners. Students speak 56 different languages and hail from 160 countries. The district has 174 elementary schools, 44 K–8 centers, 54 middle schools, 52 high schools, 4 schools with other grade configurations, and 12 alternative/special education schools.

The county includes 2.5 million of the state's approximately 20 million residents, and Miami-Dade Public Schools is the top public employer. In the private sector, construction along with accommodations and food service is the most common occupation.

evaluation. The department's guiding principles make its priorities clear (bold added):

- The difference in **teacher quality** is the strongest factor affecting student achievement.
- **Leadership** effectiveness is second to teacher quality as it relates to impact on student achievement.
- An **evaluation system that fosters teacher learning** will differ from one whose aim is to measure teacher competence.
- Increasing the effectiveness of **professional development is the leverage point** with the greatest potential for refining the day-to-day performance of educators.

"We're trying to integrate all the (branches) to say that it's a spiral," Wandarece Ruan, administrative director for professional development, said. "That if you have well trained leaders, they directly affect the quality of instruction when they evaluate teachers. Through that evaluation process, they can determine what professional development those teachers need or the school may need in order to ensure that student achievement is continuously growing."

Ruan said district leaders are focusing on changing the mindset about professional learning by connecting it to student achievement. "We know, especially through research, that learning is not sustained if it's just sit-and-get, if there isn't follow-up, if there isn't follow through, if it's not continuous," she said. "And you can't do that by just going in the district registration system, finding a course, driving there, sitting in the course, turning in the assignments, and that's it. We have to make sure that learning is job-embedded and that the connections are continuously made in teachers' minds between professional development and student outcomes."

FOCUSING ON THE DATA

Weisman said the focus on outcomes begins with student data.

"We knew we had pockets of excellence," Weisman said, "and we had a lot of data where schools were outperforming what their demographics would have predicted, but we really didn't have any coherence around the data" when the school board hired Carvalho as superintendent in 2008.

So leaders developed what they call "datacom," an accountability system that provides information by school and grade level, "down to the teacher in the class" in a graphic format.

Weisman said cabinet-level administrators regularly review the data and discuss with small groups of thirty to forty school leaders the reasons behind any changes in student outcomes—and look for areas of above average performance and external factors that influence the learning environment. If a school is performing well on a particular standard or benchmark, the principal explains to others in the room what might be happening at the school to cause it.

"We really started shifting the focus of the conversation to deliberate practice," Weisman said. "It's not so much that you brought Jane Smith into your school; it's what did Jane Smith do? We all can't have Jane Smith, but we need to know what Jane Smith was doing so that we can train other teachers to be like Jane Smith or so that Jane Smith can train other teachers in the schools with the same student population."

Datacom leads principals to own their own data. "It basically takes excuses out of the ballpark," Weisman said, "and whatever the school says at that table they need, the district is able to provide."

Ruan said the district uses student achievement data to group schools into tiers in order to determine what level of support they need to raise achievement.

"We try to provide a certain level of services for all of the schools," Ruan said, "but the needier schools receive a much higher level of direct services from the district." She said services include monitoring visits, district-level coaches, and dedicated school-based coaches. The neediest schools are assigned at least one reading coach, a math coach, and a science coach to each building. The number of schools in that tier varies each year, but is approximately sixty to seventy, Ruan said.

The district also has used incentive grants to provide intense professional development for staff in schools at this tier, hiring substitutes to release teachers or stipends for teachers to attend outside the school day. Each time students take a common assessment, the data are analyzed and used to drive instruction. The district then used $55 million from Race to the Top funding to provide bonuses to teachers who improved student outcomes.

"The carrot works better than the stick," Ruan said. "You just want them to see success. Once they get it, you just hope that it will be so enriching that they will buy into (changing their practice) and they will love it and they will continue even without the incentive."

Another tier receives some additional resources, and the higher-performing schools' data are monitored by regional administrators who meet with principals to discuss student outcomes. They may receive some regional support, such as access to assistant principals or coaches to conduct instructional reviews and provide recommendations on best practices from an outside perspective.

"Probably what has made the biggest difference is how we look at data, how we tier schools to try to provide resources and assistance to the ones that need it the most," Ruan said. "We try to provide something for everyone even if it's just peer review, but we really try to home in on the neediest and see what we can do."

FOCUSING ON SOLUTIONS

With only two required full days of professional development, the district has increasingly moved professional learning toward a job-embedded approach, creating structures that support school-based teacher learning. Schools determine what their faculties need and work to set up professional development to address those needs. Several structures aid in assuring that buildings focus on continual learning.

Professional Development
Liaisons for District Training

At the school level, each principal selects a school professional development liaison, a position created to help school staff access timely, relevant, research-based, results-oriented professional learning. Liaisons, who are paid a small stipend, coordinate site-based learning between the school, the district's regional offices, and the central office.

The liaison gets staff input on learning needs and proposes professional development to district personnel, helping to plan learning opportunities that support the school's goals and objectives. Liaisons prepare, review, and submit proposals through the district's professional development registration system for school-based professional development sessions.

The liaison also may lead professional learning and model teaching and learning. For example, he or she supports teachers by facilitating professional learning communities or acting as a resource for action research. The liaison is responsible for following up on the school's professional development plan and maintains online records for staff participants.

To support the liaisons, the district involves them in two days of training at the start of each year and sets regional monthly learning communities for them to network to share insights and best practices.

Professional Development Support Teams

Each school establishes a professional learning team, including the liaison, the principal or assistant principal, and two teacher leaders whom the principal selects. The professional learning team drives change in professional learning practices at the school.

Team members review data and survey the staff to identify learning needs, then collaborate with the principal to develop and implement a high-quality, site-based professional development plan that, according to the district,

- promotes a school culture of professional growth and collective responsibility for student learning;
- enhances educators' professional growth and effectiveness; and
- positively impacts student achievement.

The team sets the timeline and professional development calendars for their schools, including detailed plans for professional learning communities that are submitted to the district office. Central office administrators review the plans and offer feedback, proposing outcomes and helping teams make the connection between teacher learning and student achievement.

The team makes sure that teachers are collaborating, monitors learning for fidelity, and evaluates the success of professional learning, looking for its effect on student achievement.

Professional Learning Communities (PLCs)

District-level staff trained professional development team members in how to establish professional learning communities, protocols for PLCs, how to conduct lesson studies and book studies, and other professional development designs, using the teams to push learning out to the school level. The professional development teams created detailed plans for PLCs, including who would be involved, work plans, protocols they use, and expected student outcomes, then submitted the plans to the district office for review and feedback.

The school's professional development team is responsible for finding time for teachers to meet together. The district does not establish time for learning communities, although all elementary school students are dismissed at 1:50 p.m. rather than 3:20 p.m. each Wednesday to allow teachers the time to meet together, and schools may opt to use that time period for teacher collaboration. Secondary schools have designated early release days throughout the year that can be used for teacher collaboration. Some principals designate one of two monthly faculty meetings for teachers' collaboration, while others ask teachers to get together before or after school.

Central administrators visit schools to follow up and observe.

Center for Professional Learning

The district has signaled its commitment to professional learning throughout the Great Recession, continuing funding for a center for teachers to gather for professional development and to identify research-based practices. The center, founded several decades ago, was one of the first in the country and was lauded by The National Foundation for the Improvement of Education (2000) for its effectiveness. The center's effectiveness is credited to support from the teachers association, university involvement, and ongoing commitment to its operation. Center staff members also spend time in schools, tailoring professional development to the needs that schools have identified.

Teacher Evaluations

The district has begun a new evaluation system that rates professional performance using student outcomes. However, rather than a punitive approach, leaders are emphasizing using evaluations as feedback for continual learning. The district must invest in teacher professional learning, Weisman said. Miami is a major metropolitan area located at the bottom of a peninsula and has few places from which to draw a new workforce. "Our workforce is our workforce," she said. "It's not like we can go to neighboring townships and get employees, be they teachers or bus drivers."

The district is working with school administrators on what to look for in teacher observations and how to link those observations to support through professional learning.

Software that was put into place for the 2014–15 school year will enable administrators to recommend district training, teachers to sign up for courses online, and the district to record teachers' "PD history," which then can be reflected in teacher evaluations. The database allows administrators to recommend district course offerings for teachers based on their observations, for example, recommending more professional development on differentiating instruction. Information then is sent to the teacher showing what professional development is available and when. The online system tracks information on when walk-throughs occurred, evaluator recommendations, what professional development the teacher participated in, and what results occurred in improving student achievement.

"It's not just that you're evaluating them for the purpose of an end-of-the-year summary," Ruan said. "You're evaluating them to give them productive feedback on possible professional development that would help them be better at what they're doing and to make sure that what they're doing is quality."

Professional Learning in Practice: Norwood Elementary

It was twenty minutes before the morning bell at Norwood Elementary School and already the math coach had popped her head into Jennifer Garcia's fourth-grade room to check on her. Garcia had taught her class a math lesson the prior day, and as students completed practice problems, she looked over their shoulders to see who grasped the concept and which students didn't understand.

"No matter how many times you tell them, 'Tell me if you don't understand,'" Garcia said, "they don't really like to say it."

So if a student missed one of two questions marked as indicators of understanding in the text, a strategy she and the coach had discussed, Garcia did a quick intervention to help the child get on track. If a student had both questions wrong, she made a note. She would group those students for a follow-up lesson to make sure they were keeping up. Now, the math coach arranged to visit the class to help those students who needed additional follow-up.

> The mission of Norwood Elementary School is to provide an environment which will prepare all students to be academically, socially, and physically successful in meeting the challenges of a multicultural society through technology, appropriate instructional strategies, self-discipline, and parental and community support.

That kind of support, along with support from the school administration, has helped the teachers at Norwood improve outcomes for students. This school, where nine out of ten students live in poverty, earned A's on its state report card in eight of the last ten years.

Norwood is a pre-K through fifth-grade building of roughly five hundred students about sixteen miles northwest of downtown Miami—almost in the shadow of Sun Life Stadium, the home of the Miami Dolphins football team. The school is formally part of the city of Miami Gardens, created when Interstate 95 was built and displaced many, mainly low-income families and is the largest predominantly African-American city in Florida. Norwood's student population is 99 percent African-American.

The school building sits between the Florida Turnpike and a neighborhood of single-story, 1,500 square-foot, three-bedroom stucco homes where most of its students lived in the past. Teachers note that generations of families attended Norwood; they would see sibling groups, cousins, children of students they once taught. Now, Norwood is facing new challenges as deeper poverty infiltrates the school. Some neighborhood homes have become government housing. At the same time, new standards are raising the bar, Garcia said, and the value placed on education is lessening. Garcia said the new standards and more rigorous requirements challenge educators, making ongoing professional learning a necessity.

"There is this culture of competitiveness, but not amongst ourselves really or against our peers, or even necessarily with other schools," Garcia said. "I mean competitive like we just want to see our students succeed. You really want *all* the students to succeed. And for them to do better, we have to do better."

Norwood has developed a culture in which teachers focus more intently on students, continually examining student data, sharing what works, and getting support from the administration through feedback and help with the students from reading, math, and science coaches, as well as the principal himself.

"So the culture is share, care, and everybody will be better, including ourselves," Garcia said. "That has helped us push and stay at a high level."

Once a week, teachers meet with their grade-level colleagues during common planning time. While they have an hour each day for planning, Principal Kevin Williams requires one day of collaboration during this time. He said these meetings are coordinated by a grade-level chairperson, and either he, an assistant principal, or a coach attends to support teachers in planning the next instructional units.

For example, fourth-grade teachers at Norwood Elementary looked at students' reading baselines in one grade-level team meeting. They examined data for their individual classes and then strategized ways to address identified weak areas. They suggested possible resources, and took questions that couldn't be resolved to an all-faculty "conversation" later that week.

At least once each month, faculty have "professional conversations" as a whole group during their regular meeting time after school for an hour to an hour and a half of learning. They might discuss a new instructional approach, learn more about a district mandate, or divide into grade-level groups for conversations about a focus leaders have identified. Some staff voluntarily took part in unpaid "professional conversations" before the start of the school year that focused on barriers keeping students from reaching the higher standards.

"We have professional conversations that help us to improve our instruction within our classroom," teacher Nicole Ferguson said. "We talk about best practices and how we can help our kids reach their goals, and we model different strategies that we can use to improve our students' learning."

Then, Williams spends half of his day in classrooms letting teachers know what he sees that he believes is effective and what might be improved on—but always with the spirit of "we're all in this together." That feeling of support rather than recrimination is essential to improvement, teachers said.

Williams looks for implementation. For example, the faculty focused on one standard to be taught in the upcoming week, and he looked in on classes to see that the teachers had posted an essential question for students to see. He focuses his conversation with teachers on a single, identified aspect at any particular time. In another example, Williams asked teachers to create a poster of what a rigorous classroom "looks like, feels like, and sounds like" and then had groups present and discuss the results before he arrived in their classrooms looking for the attributes they had identified.

"I can't place an expectation on my teachers if I'm not constantly inspecting what they're doing," Williams said of the hours each day he spends in classrooms. "It's not for the purpose of being punitive, but for the purpose of how I can assist and how I can help them. You won't know what to provide them with if you're not viewing what's going on."

Williams, teachers say, sees himself as the "head teacher" in the school, giving—and receiving—advice. In his classroom visits, he might pull a group of students to tutor in a short lesson to help the teacher continue with the rest of the class. He might send a coach into that room, or find another resource. He might teach a class so the teacher can observe another colleague who has a particularly effective way of explaining a concept to a class.

"I think (regular observation) builds that culture," Williams said. "The teachers, parents, and students know that you're here, that you're visible, and they know you have their best interest at heart. With any instructional leader, *they* have to be priority. All of the other stuff can wait."

He reallocated his staff and funding to ensure that teachers have the coaches they need. As a high-performing school in the district, he does not receive some of the extra funding that is used to target the lower performing buildings. Williams used discretionary Title 1 funding to hire a full-time reading coach and then scheduled coaching time for math and science teacher leaders, whose duties are reduced from having their own class to co-teaching along with providing support.

"That's exactly how professional development helps students in the long run—when student outcomes are foremost in your mind, you're not judgmental, and you just say, 'let's work together to figure this out,'" Garcia said. "When you're about the students, you don't mind sharing; you don't mind asking." Ferguson noted that the coaches also model by attending coaches' meetings to further their own learning. She said the culture of teamwork and support pushes teachers to continually learn how to help students achieve.

She emphasized the cycle of continually examining data and following up with professional conversations about addressing student learning needs as the answer to improving outcomes. Garcia said collaboration is essential to improving student outcomes.

"It's being able to discuss what works academically, socially, organizationally with other teachers that has the greatest impact on me as a teacher," Garcia said.

Garcia and Ferguson both research best practices online on their own and seek outside opportunities—whatever it takes to continue to push themselves to improve their practice.

"As we learn, even if we don't mean to I think it just overflows out of us into the classroom," Garcia said. "We might change our ways or enhance what we do."

"Professional learning gives us a chance to embrace change even when a lot of people don't want to embrace change—because that's human nature," Garcia continued. "As we grow we can't help but bring it back into the classroom. And that's the whole point of teaching—learning never stops. If you think you have no learning to do as a teacher, I don't see how you could be a good teacher. It's constant learning for us, and constant learning for our students."

Figure 3.1 Miami-Dade Trial Urban District Assessment (TUDA) results compared with large city scores

			Average district score	Average score for large city	District percent at or above basic
MATH	**4th grade**	2013	237*	235	81
		2011	236	233	79
		2009	236	231	81
	8th grade	2013	274*	276	63*
		2011	272*	274	61*
		2009	273*	271	64
READING	**4th grade**	2013	223	212	70
		2011	221	211	67
		2009	221	210	68
	8th grade	2013	259*	258	71*
		2011	260	255	71
		2009	261	252	73
SCIENCE	**4th grade**	2009	144	135	66
	8th grade	2009	137	134	49

Shaded cells indicate results that are higher than large city results.
*indicates scores that are not significantly different from large city results.

Source: Institute of Education Sciences and National Center for Education Statistics (2011).

VIEW FROM THREE SEATS

Jennifer Garcia

Teacher Leader, Norwood Elementary School

I think you have to take responsibility personally for your professional learning. For example, when we had a new standard that students were required to meet that was not covered in our textbook, I did research online on my own and printed out materials that would help students meet that standard. I attend workshops, of course those mandated by the school, but also sometimes on my own in the summer. New things are always popping up. You have to take responsibility yourself even before you rely on the school for your learning.

Teachers aren't always given time for professional learning. The only way to do this job is to make the time. I make time to plan vertically with other math teachers. As a fourth-grade teacher, I see the third-grade math teacher or the fifth-grade math teacher every two weeks at least so that we can talk if I noticed some students who aren't doing very well on a particular strand. Or, we discuss what areas students are having trouble with and where we see students struggling so that we can make adjustments at our grade levels. Planning time no longer is just grading papers and tasks like that. We really have to delve into the lessons together. That kind of collaboration occurs here schoolwide.

We take very seriously talking with each other and sharing best practices. It doesn't matter how long you've been teaching—we all have something to bring to the table. This is my first year of teaching just math and science, and it's helped me to have discussions with other teachers of those subjects, asking, "What did you do?" I don't feel at all bad asking another teacher or a coach, "How did you do this? Because my students are having problems with it." Maybe the way I'm teaching it is not bad, but for some reason they're not getting it. As a teacher, you have to grow up and recognize that we're only human. You have to say to yourself, "This is not about me."

Wandarece Ruan

Administrative director, professional development

From the district office, you have a completely different perspective of what quality professional development actually is and how it affects what teachers do, how they do it, and how well they do it. There has been a paradigm shift in professional development; it's not just about having the opportunity to take courses to make sure that you can extend your certificate. The purpose of professional learning is a lot larger than "This is a way for me to gain master plan points so that I don't have to go out

(Continued)

(Continued)

to the university and pay for a class" or "I'm doing this so that I can pass my observations and at the end of the year, perhaps I'll get a bonus." All of professional learning has to be directly related to effective instruction.

What we in this office try to focus on is to take three pieces—professional development, leadership development, and evaluation—and connect them all to a framework. So that, for example, the evaluation is not to determine whether or not I continue employment, to determine whether or not I'm eligible for a bonus, but is connected to effective instruction. We want to tailor our message so that that is what our framework really is about—that everything that we do is tied directly to effective instruction. That's the beginning of the outcome; if we are effective in our instruction, the outcome will be better student achievement. We're trying to change the mindset and the way that people think, trying to change the way that people teach, the way that people look at and view professional learning and trying to help them see how huge an impact that it has in the classroom.

As educators, we need to continuously grow professionally so that we can continue to be good at what we do and can continue to positively affect the learning of students in our classrooms. We want teachers to see that learning begins with them in their buildings. Our message to them is it starts there with you.

Kevin Williams

Principal, Norwood Elementary School

This year I have several coaches who are classroom teachers, but we worked it out so they are able to assist and model throughout the day in different classes what in-depth instruction needs to look like. In addition, teachers have common planning time, and so during that common planning time, they're shown what in-depth planning looks like because you can't just wing it anymore. Teachers must plan in-depth to cover every component of the standards.

On our professional development days set for us by the district, we strategically plan what is going to be presented so it's not just doing professional development to do professional development. Anybody at the school can take a workshop, but we want to make sure we are targeting learning needs. For example, we noticed our teachers needed to unwrap the standards, to really delve into them. What is this standard really saying I need to be doing? So in a professional conversation, we took one standard and teachers separated into groups by grade level to find the key words in the standard. Then they talked about what this would look like in a classroom.

As principal, I also model activities. For example, I did an activity in which I modeled and said to the teachers, "This kind of modeling is what I should be seeing when I walk through your classroom, because I'm doing this to show you what you should be doing so it's not just me telling you. I am treating you like you're a student in my class, and here's my expectation of you. I'm doing it with the end in mind. My expectation is that when we end this conversation, you should know this, this, and this."

We have targeted, focused discussions and professional development, not just to do sessions, but to make sure that learning is happening based on our particular needs in our school rather than only what the state says we have to do. There are some components that we are wonderful at, so there's no sense to keep beating that horse. We look at what *we* need, and that's where we target our professional learning.

CASE STUDY DISCUSSION QUESTIONS

1. The Outcomes Standard identifies three key components: a) meeting educator performance standards, b) addressing student learning outcomes, and c) building coherence. [See Standard rationale at the beginning of the book for more detail.] Identify elements from the case study that address each of these key components. Were some components addressed more deeply than others in the district?

2. How was the focus on student and educator outcomes emphasized in the budget process described at the beginning of the case study? What other ways did district staff stress the importance of student learning and professional development?

3. The district focused on building "human capital." Examine the four guiding principles and discuss how these principles might be put into action. For example, how would the district, school, or principal demonstrate that **teacher quality is the strongest factor affecting student achievement?**

4. In what ways did central office actions, policies, and programs cement the connection between professional learning and effective instruction?

5. What is your reaction to the tiered support system used by Miami-Dade—providing differentiated support to schools based on need? How could that system promote student and teacher outcomes? How could that system deter student and teacher outcomes?

6. How do teacher evaluations build upon the district's and school's emphasis on student outcomes, professional learning, and effective instruction? How might the evaluation system be refined to place teacher learning—not just professional learning participation—into sharper focus?

7. Review the description of a meeting of fourth-grade teachers at Norwood Elementary School. Would these conversations be typical of your school or not? What kinds of relationships and trust would be needed to discuss these topics in your school?

8. The principal at Norwood Elementary School seems to spend a lot of time in classrooms. How would those observations and debriefings support the accomplishment of student and educator outcomes?

9. Kevin Williams, the principal at Norwood Elementary School, states that teachers needed to *unwrap the standards— really delve into them.* What do you think he saw, heard, or analyzed to cause him to identify that specific teacher learning need in his school?

REFERENCES

Adams, C. (2013, Winter). The fantastic five. *Scholastic Administrator, Back-to-School Issue.* Retrieved from http://www.scholastic.com/browse/article.jsp?id=3758194

College Board. (2014, January 29). *Miami-Dade County Public Schools named the College Board's advanced placement district of the year.* Retrieved from https://www.collegeboard.org/releases/2014/miami-dade-county-public-schools-named-college-boards-advanced-placement-district-year

D'Orio, W. (n.d.). Profile: Alberto Carvalho. *Scholastic Administrator.* Retrieved from http://www.scholastic.com/browse/article.jsp?id= 3756759

Institute of Education Sciences. (2011). *National assessment of educational progress.* Washington, DC: U.S. Department of Education. Retrieved from http://nces.ed.gov/nationsreportcard/districts/

Maxwell, L. A. (2014, August 20). U.S. school enrollment hits majority-minority milestone. *Education Week, 34*(1), 1, 12, 14–15. Retrieved from http://www.edweek.org/ew/articles/2014/08/20/01demographics .h34.html

Miami-Dade County Public Schools. (2013–2014). *Statistical highlights.* Miami, FL: Author. Retrieved from http://oada.dadeschools.net/ SH1314.pdf

National Center for Education Statistics. (2011). District profiles. Retrieved from http://nces.ed.gov/nationsreportcard/districts/

National Center for Education Statistics. (2014). *Selected statistics from the public elementary and secondary education universe: School year 2012–13.* Retrieved from http://nces.ed.gov/pubs2014/2014098.pdf

The National Foundation for the Improvement of Education. (2000, Summer). Creating teacher-led professional development centers. Retrieved from https://www.neafoundation.org/downloads/NEA-Creating_Teacher-Led_Prof_Dev.pdf

Rosen, P. (2011, March/April). Miami-Dade Superintendent Alberto Carvalho. *Education Update.* Retrieved from www.educationupdate .com/archives/2011/MAR/html/spot-miami.html

Appendix

Professional Learning Planning Checklist

PART A: Professional Development Standards

CONTEXT: The context refers to "how" the organization is set up and the culture of the school. Creating context is an ongoing process. The first step is to organize staff into professional learning communities whose goals are aligned with those of the school and with district initiatives.

_____ organizes adults into learning communities that have goals in alignment with the school and District

_____ requires skillful school and District leaders to guide continuous instructional improvement

_____ requires resources to support adult learning and collaboration

PROCESS: The process refers to the "how" of professional development—namely, the type and forms of professional learning activities and the way those activities are planned, organized, implemented, and followed up.

_____ applies disaggregated student data to determine adult learning priorities, monitor progress, and sustain continuous improvement

_____ uses multiple sources of evaluation information to guide improvement and demonstrate its impact

_____ prepares educators to apply research to decision making

_____ designs learning strategies appropriate to the intended goal

_____ applies knowledge about human learning and change

_____ provides educators with knowledge and skills to collaborate

CONTENT: The content refers to the "what" of professional development. What is it that the entire faculty needs, even if different processes are used? What is it that students must know and be able to do?

_____ prepares educators to understand and appreciate all students (equity); create safe, orderly, and supportive learning environments; and set high expectations for their academic achievement

_____ deepens educators' content knowledge, provides research-based instructional strategies to assist educators in helping students meet rigorous academic standards, and prepares them to use various types of classroom assessments appropriately (quality teaching)

_____ provides knowledge and skills to help educators involve families and other stakeholders

PART B: Goals, Objectives, and Desired Outcomes

1. Identify the strategic goal(s) or school improvement plan area(s) to be addressed by this professional development activity.

_____

_____

_____

_____

_____

_____

2. What are the specific desired outcomes for this activity relating to anticipated changes in the participants? Identify outcomes for at least one indicator of change:

A. Knowledge:

_____

_____

B. Attitudes:

_____

_____

C. Skills:

_____

_____

D. Aspirations:

_____

_____

E. Behaviors:

_____

_____

PART C: Data Analysis

1. What data were reviewed to determine the need for this activity? (Multiple sets of data should be reviewed, including educator and student data.)

_____

_____

2. What data will be gathered in order to evaluate the effectiveness and impact of this activity?

_____

_____

PART D: Identify Resources

    1. Fiscal:

_____

_____

    2. Human:

_____

_____

    3. Other:

_____

_____

PART E: Follow-Up

    1. What follow-up activities will be used to support ongoing professional learning (e.g., face-to-face, online modules, learning teams)?

_____

_____

_____

_____

    2. How will follow-up be scheduled?

Follow-Up Activity	Person(s) Responsible	Timeline	Evaluation of Follow-Up

PART F: Evaluation

What measures will you use to assess whether the activity enabled the school to meet its goal? Evaluate the achievement of objectives at the school, team, and grade levels. What are the indicators demonstrating successful application of the knowledge or skills in the classroom to promote student achievement?

_____

_____

_____

_____

PART G: Continuous Planning

What are the next steps with respect to the specific activity—continue, modify, and repeat the activity?

_____

_____

_____

_____

Index

CORWIN

A SAGE Company

Helping educators make the greatest impact

CORWIN HAS ONE MISSION: to enhance education through intentional professional learning.

We build long-term relationships with our authors, educators, clients, and associations who partner with us to develop and continuously improve the best evidence-based practices that establish and support lifelong learning.

learningforward

Advancing professional learning for student success

Learning Forward (formerly National Staff Development Council) is an international association of learning educators committed to one purpose in K–12 education: Every educator engages in effective professional learning every day so every student achieves.